Stop Motion Handbook 3.1
using GarageBand and iStopMotion

Craig Lauridsen

Stop Motion Handbook 3.1 *(second edition)*

Craig Lauridsen

First published 2012, this edition 2016

© 2016 Craig Lauridsen
Acumen
19 Trevor Terrace, Newtown
Wellington 6021
New Zealand

ISBN 978-0-473-33886-2

Also available in colour: ISBN (978-0-473-33980-7)

> **The website for this book is *stop-motion-handbook.com***
> Go to the website to: BUY the iStopMotion software, BUY the ebook (ISBN 978-0-473-33887-9) or CONTACT the author.
> For information on creating stop motion entirely on an iPad go to ***ipadanimation.net***

Notice of Rights

This material is the property of the author and cannot be reproduced in any form without the written permission of the writer. Contact the writer at *smbook@acumen.net.nz*

Notice of Liability

The information in this book is distributed on an 'As Is' basis without warranty. While every precaution has been taken in the preparation of this book the author has no liability to any person or entity with respect to loss or damage caused or alleged to be caused directly or indirectly by the instructions contained in this book, or by the computer software and hardware products described in it.

Trademarks

GarageBand, iMovie, iPhoto, iTunes, iPhone, iPad and iPod are trademarks of Apple Inc., registered in the US and other countries.

Boinx and iStopMotion are trademarks of Boinx Software Ltd.

LEGO is a trademark of The LEGO Group.

Plasticine is a trademark of Flair Leisure Products plc.

Average Joe is property of Newtown Movie School.

Stop Motion

Fast track the learning curve to making your own stop motion movies. **It's fun, it's crazy, it's addictive.** The Stop Motion Handbook leads you through simple and robust processes, helping both beginner and amateur animators make good decisions when creating stop motion.

By avoiding the common mistakes, your first movies will have the quality of a more seasoned movie maker. This is a great guide for teachers, parents, children, amateur movie makers and anyone who wants to produce their own stop motion.

By using this book, you'll learn the key competencies across a broad range of learning areas:

- Developing a story and writing it into a SCRIPT
- Recording the AUDIO of the script (dialogue, sound effects and music) in GarageBand, and saving it as a soundtrack
- Making PROPS and BACKGROUNDS and creating the CHARACTERS to bring your story to life
- Recording the stop motion PICTURES in iStopMotion
- EDITING the movie, if required, adding a title and credits in iMovie.

This book is an accessible reference resource; read it cover to cover, or dive into a specific topic and work through the step by step guidelines. While the book covers many universal principles of stop motion, the step by step examples refer to iStopMotion *(www.boinx.com)*, GarageBand and iMovie *(www.apple.com)* – all Mac software.

Many of the examples used have been produced by children so are easily accessible and affordable.

The Newtown Movie School provides fully interactive stop motion movie making workshops for children. This book is our reference guide and has been published to assist young animators and teachers worldwide.

Craig Lauridsen

Also by Craig Lauridsen

Available from *www.ipadanimation.net*

iPad Animation

How to make stop motion movies on the iPad with GarageBand, iStopMotion and iMovie

Contains more than 230 pages of instruction, tips, examples and flow chart diagrams so you can master stop motion – fast!

iPad Animation covers 4 apps (iStopMotion, Garageband, iMovie and djay), 9 stop motion projects and 15 accessories and includes 50 movie and sound examples.

Register your copy of iPad Animation and download 29 bonus soundtracks.

Also available as an ebook and interactive iBook.

Creating a Stop Motion Story

Unlock your Imagination

A straightforward step-by-step guide to creating a story-driven stop motion movie. Ideal for the classroom and hobby.

Create a complete movie of an original story in a few hours.

3 apps, one iPad, 100% creativity.

An excellent digital media resource for teachers and students.

Also available as an ebook.

Contents

QUICK START	**1**
What is stop motion?	1
Recording the audio first	**2**
Recording the pictures first	**4**
Power tips for making better stop motion	**5**
OVERVIEW	**9**
Methods of stop motion	**10**
What equipment do I need?	12
File names	12
SCRIPT	**15**
What makes a great movie?	**16**
Different types of stories – genres	17
Developing the story	**18**
Writing a script	**19**
Step 1: Writing a premise	19
Step 2: Questions which develop the premise	19
Step 3: Writing the story outline	20
Step 4: Writing the story into a script	23
Adapting a story for a script	**24**
Improvising a script	**26**
Tips to develop a story	**27**
Writing a TV advertisement	**31**
AUDIO	**33**
Microphones	34
Equipment to record sound	35
GarageBand	**36**
Creating a soundtrack	**40**
Step 1: Recording the dialogue	41
Sound recording process	42

Step 2: Reviewing the dialogue timing	43
Step 3: Adding sound effects	44
Step 4: Adding ambience sounds	44
Step 5: Adding music	44
Step 6: Adjust the volume	46
Step 7: Apply effects	46
Step 8: Finalising the soundtrack	49
Step 9: Saving the soundtrack	50

Recording with a microphone — 51
Sound versus noise — 56
Tips for great sound — 57
   How to make a microphone 'shock' mount — 59
Adding other media — 60
   Getting additional sound effects and music — 60
   Sound effects — 61
   Music — 63
Adding loops — 65
Software Instruments — 67
Editing the soundtrack — 68

PROPS AND SET UP — 73

Modelling with Plasticine — 74
   Plasticine modelling tools — 74
   Making an armature Plasticine character — 75
   2D Plasticine characters — 78
Building with LEGO — 79
Setting up a stop motion stage — 80
   Standard stage with painted background — 80
   Invisible horizon stage — 81
   Green screen stage — 82
   Flat stage — 83
Creating a three dimensional world — 84
Tips for great pictures — 86
   Picture composition — 86
   The 'rule of thirds' — 87
   Action safe — 88

Camera angle	88
Camera focus	89
Behind the scenes	92

Camera, tripod and mount — 94
Choosing a camera for stop motion	94
Camera tripod	97
How to make a camera mount	98
How to make a remote camera mount	99

Lighting — 100
How to make a portable stage — 104

PICTURES — 107

iStopMotion — 108
Picture size (Preset)	108
Picture rate (Frame rate)	109
Time lapse	112
The iStopMotion window	113

Making a stop motion — 115
Step 1: Opening iStopMotion	115
Step 2: Choosing the camera	116
Step 3: Importing soundtrack	118
Step 4: Recording your first picture	119
Animation process	120
Step 5: Bringing your characters to life	121
Rule 1 and 2	122
Step 6: Playing your stop motion	123
Step 7: Editing your stop motion	126
Step 8: Saving your stop motion	126

View options — 127
Importing a reference video	128
Making a LEGO minifigure walk	130
Using replacement figures	132
Making a character talk	132

Creating visual effects — 136
How to dramatise an action sequence	143
How to create an epic stop motion movie	145
Illustration animation	146

Whiteboard animation	147
Flat 2D animation	148
Two level stop motion	149
Time lapse – security system	150
Tilt shift - miniatures	151

Common stop motion mistakes — 152

Advanced iStopMotion — 155

Compositing pane	155
Editing pictures	157
Stop motion with a digital still camera	159
Planning a complex stop motion	163

Principles of animation — 164

EDIT AND PUBLISH — 169

iMovie — 170

Editing stop motion clip to make a movie — 171

Adding titles	172
Play the movie	174
Adding other movie elements	174
Assembling a larger stop motion project	179

Saving the movie — 180

Websites for more information	181

Premiere — 182

INDEX — 184

TEACHER LESSON PLANS — 189

Thanks

These people have been integral in bringing this book to reality.

Jamin Vollebregt – the last few years with Newtown Movie School have been a great movie making adventure with you. You've been there from the beginning. Your creative and practical ideas have given many kids incredible movie making experiences and helped to develop this book into a unique educational reference.

Mae Manalansan – for a thousand and one support tasks from clearcutting images to converting this book to the EPUB version.

Tino Tezel, Sarah Schwaiger and Oliver Breidenbach from Boinx – for coming on board with your encouragement. It is always easier to do things with a team behind you.

James, Fiona and Tane Hippolite, Al Kinley, Inshirah Mahal and Sam Wadham – for putting their hands up as proofreaders and giving a wide range of valuable feedback.

Malcolm Shearer – for your meticulous proofing of all the software instructions at a point when I couldn't see the wood for the trees and needed a fresh set of eyes.

Teachers Ben Gittos, Sarah Taverner, Kelvin Harper, Kirsty Stewart, Hilary Hague and Principal Sandra McCallum – for your feedback on using this book in schools.

Ian Adams – for your cover and page design. As always, a fabulous job.

Ros Jaquiery – for meticulous proofing of so many versions.

And lastly, thank you to the B-SMART team (Brayden, Sara, Matthew, Amy, Reuben and Theo) and all the children who have attended Newtown Movie School and given insight and feedback about the best ways to make stop motion movies.

Craig

Quick start

Conventions

This handbook gives direct instruction for using computer software. References such as 'File⇢Save' mean go to the 'File' menu and select 'Save' from the drop down list.

iStopMotion	File	Edit	Source	Movie	View
New	⌘N
Open...	⌘O
Open Recent	▶
Close	⌘W
Save	⌘S
Save As...	⇧⌘S
Document Settings...	⌘;
Export...	⌘E
Export as GIF...	
Export Selection	▶
Send to Final Cut Pro	⌥F
Send to iMovie	⌥I
Page Setup...	⇧⌘P
Print Flip Book...	⌘P

What is stop motion?

Stop motion is a movie made from a series of individual pictures. When the pictures are viewed one after the other, our eyes are 'tricked' into thinking that the objects in the pictures are moving. This is the magic of stop motion.

In this book, we use iStopMotion software *(www.boinx.com)*, Apple's GarageBand and iMovie software *(www.apple.com)* to make stop motion.

This chapter is written for those who just want to dive in and get started. If you want more detail, follow the page numbers to the appropriate sections.

This chapter outlines two processes to make stop motion:

- recording the audio first, or
- recording the pictures first.

The last part of this chapter is a summary of the vital keys for a high quality movie. These are expanded more fully in the rest of this book.

Recording the audio first

The best way to make stop motion is to create the soundtrack first, then record the pictures to match. As you record the pictures you'll be able to hear and 'see' the soundtrack so you can confidently record the right number of pictures and achieve perfect alignment between character movements and the sounds. Here is an outline of a process to record the audio first.

Write story and SCRIPT
(see page 15)

Record AUDIO in GarageBand
(see page 33)

1) Record audio/create soundtrack
2) Save original GarageBand file (File⸺>Save)
3) Save soundtrack (Share⸺>Export Song to Disk)

Record PICTURES in iStopMotion
(see page 107)

1) Load soundtrack (View pane)
2) Animate and record pictures one at a time to match the audio
3) Save iStopMotion file (File⸺>Save)
4) Save movie (File⸺>Export – choose Quicktime Movie option)

EDIT movie in iMovie
(Optional step – see page 169)

1) File ⇢ Import Movies
2) Combine iStopMotion movie segments
3) Add effects, titles, credits
4) Save movie (Share to File)

Edit AUDIO in GarageBand
(Optional step – see page 33)

1) Import movie (Media Browser – Movies panel)
2) Edit audio
3) Save movie (Share ⇢ Export Movie to Disk)

Miniature Wellington
by Jared Gray

A tilt shift time lapse of my (Craig Lauridsen's) home town – 'The coolest little capital in the world', Wellington, New Zealand.
www.youtube.com/watch?v=-7wBoYFeHQI

Recording the pictures first

In some stop motion, eg time lapse, picture montage or slideshow, the pictures can be recorded first. The audio, often a voice-over narrative or simply music, can be added later as it is not likely to be timing specific. Here is an outline of a process to record the pictures first.

Record PICTURES in iStopMotion
(see page 107)

1) Record pictures one at a time directly in iStopMotion or import a batch of pictures from a still camera
2) Save iStopMotion file (File⟶Save)
3) Save movie (File⟶Export – choose Quicktime Movie option)

EDIT movie in iMovie
(see page 169)

1) File⟶Import Movies
2) Combine iStopMotion movie segments
3) Add sound effects, titles, credits
4) Save movie (Share to File)

Record AUDIO in GarageBand
(Optional step – see page 33)

1) Import movie (Media Browser – Movies panel)
2) Record audio/create soundtrack
3) Save original GarageBand file (File⟶Save)
4) Save movie (Share⟶Export Movie to Disk)

Power tips for making better stop motion

Of all the tips for making better quality stop motion, these first two tips – we call them 'rules' will make the most difference.

> **Rule 1 – Secure the camera on a tripod or mount and DON'T MOVE IT** for that scene, dialogue or action. Move only your characters around on the stage. **Moving the camera too often may produce a movie that is very jumpy, confusing and hard to watch** (page 122).
>
> **Rule 2 – MOVE THE CAMERA to a new and very different angle for a new scene, line of dialogue or action.**
> Each camera movement should **help the audience to follow the story and get more involved** in the action (page 122).

A story needs to be about something. Try this prompt to get started: **'What might happen if…?'** (page 19).

Write a script and record the soundtrack first. Then record the pictures to match (pages 15, 33 and 107).

If the sound is clear, your audience will think the picture quality is better than it is. So, **invest in better sound equipment and learn better recording techniques before you buy a better camera** (page 33).

When recording the audio, **find a quiet room and turn off all background noises** (page 56).

Mime the actions to help record the right timing between lines of dialogue and to express the right voice tone (page 43).

Reduce the distance between the microphone and the sound source to increase the sound level in relation to the surrounding noise (page 56).

Have voice actors stand so they have better voice control (page 58).

Voice actors need to **take care with pronunciation.** Record the audio again if you hear words that run together or where the diction is not clear (page 57).

The more unwanted sounds and noise you can remove from audio clips, the cleaner the soundtrack will be (page 68).

Keep your hands clean when working with Plasticine (page 74).

Secure all props and backgrounds, including LEGO® base boards, **so they can't accidentally move** during filming (page 80).

Curve a large piece of card as a one-piece stage background and base to avoid visible joins between sheets and to create a natural horizon (page 81).

Regularly check the arrangement of the characters, props and camera position for good composition (page 86).

Position the camera so that the character's eyes are one third down the screen and you'll be a long way towards having good composition (page 87).

Use the Action Safe guide to keep characters away from the edge of the screen (page 88).

To make your movie look more like a 'film' (where characters are sharp and in focus but the background is blurry) position characters much closer to the camera than to the background and **set your camera to manual focus** (page 90).

Turn off your camera's image stabiliser, if it has one, as it can affect the alignment of the pictures (page 94).

Check camera settings such as exposure and white balance (pages 96 and 116).

Use a 'close-up' or macro lens for close-up pictures (pages 94 and 95).

Securely fix the tripod or camera mount and do whatever you can to avoid accidentally moving it (page 97).

Control all lighting sources including blocking out windows. Use appropriate artificial lights with dimmers, diffusers and bounce boards to get soft and even lighting (page 100).

When you are learning, **reduce the picture rate to 12 pictures (frames) per second** (FPS). It will still give realistic motion and really speeds up the movie making process (normal speed is up to 30 FPS) (page 109).

Make sure iStopMotion's Autosave feature is on (page 115).

Accurately matching your pictures with your sound is an easy way to make your movie powerful (page 118).

Characters that are speaking should move – keep all other characters relatively still (page 132).

Wait until everyone is clear of the stage before recording each picture so that you don't get hands or unwanted shadows in the shot (page 152).

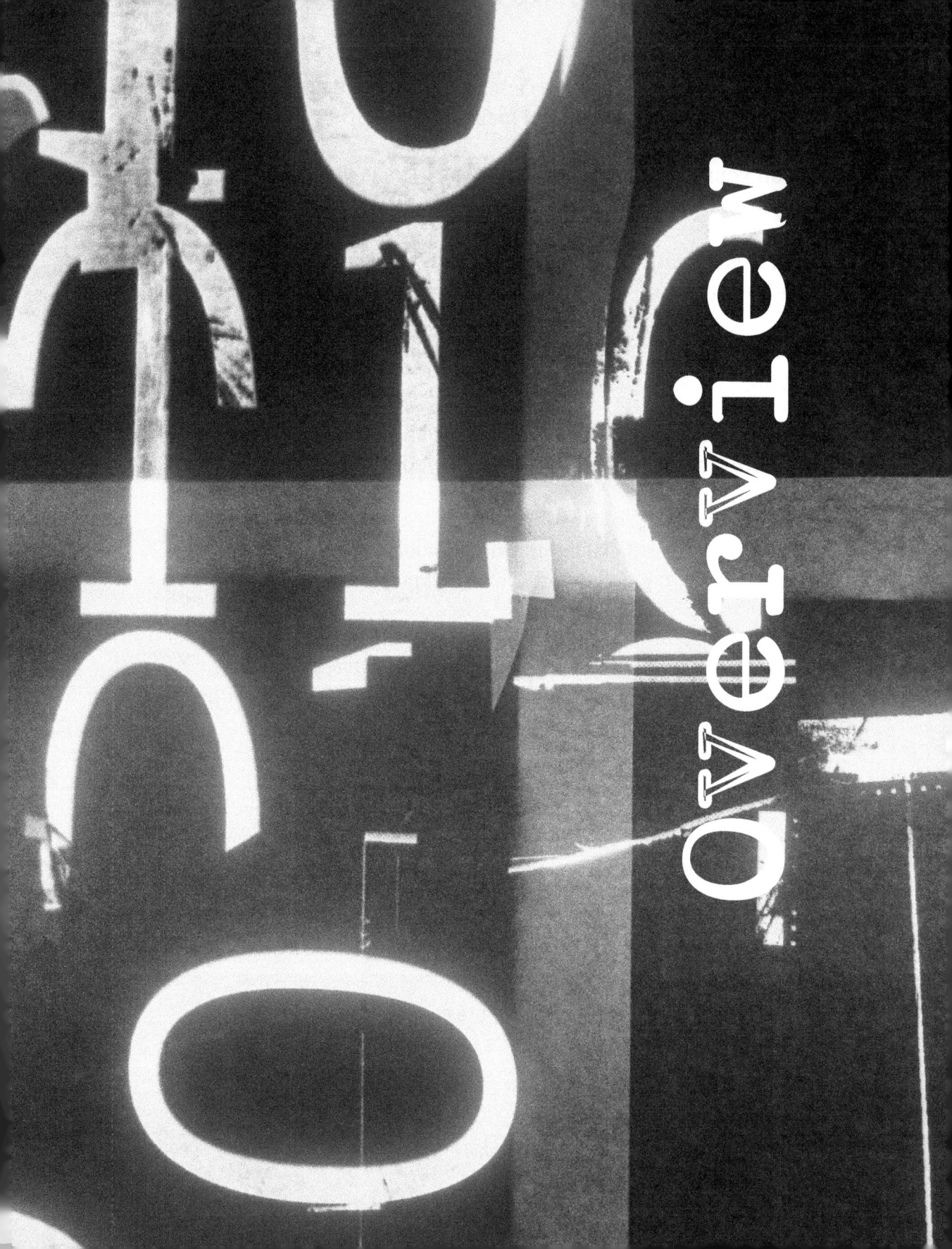

The chapters in this book cover:

- Developing a story and writing it into a **SCRIPT**
- Recording the **AUDIO** of the script (dialogue, sound effects and music) in GarageBand, and saving it as a soundtrack
- Making **PROPS** and **BACKGROUNDS** and creating the **CHARACTERS** to bring your story to life
- Recording the stop motion **PICTURES** in iStopMotion
- **EDITING** the movie (if required) and adding a title and credits in iMovie
- **PUBLISHING** your movie.

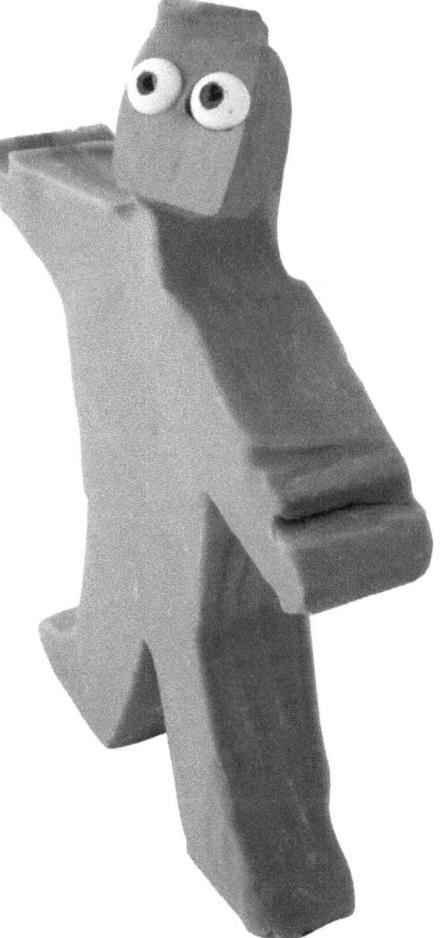

Methods of stop motion

Stop motion falls into three general categories – Brickmation, Claymation and everything else.

Brickmation

LEGO® is the most popular medium for stop motion because a huge range of minifigures and props are readily available in the same scale. LEGO® minifigures are more robust than Plasticine and won't squash, smudge or break in your hand. Minifigure bodies can make some animation movements, but not as many as Plasticine.

Claymation

Claymation or clay animation (we use **Plasticine** from an art supply shop) is probably the most traditional and best known medium for stop motion animation.

Plasticine can be moulded and shaped into anything your imagination can come up with.

There are two main types of claymation figures:

- **Armature models** which have some kind of skeletal structure, usually made of wire. The armature acts as a skeleton that supports your Plasticine and allows you to move the body limbs. Pre-made armatures can be purchased at art supply stores or you can also make your own (see *Making an armature Plasticine character* on page 75)
- **Freeform models** which do not use any internal skeletal structure.

While Plasticine is pliable, constant reshaping can weaken it. From time to time you may need to replace parts with fresh Plasticine. Extend the life of Plasticine characters by integrating solid items such as beads for eyes. Big screen stop motion movies use silicone rubber as an alternative to Plasticine.

In most situations you'll want to mould 3D figures which stand upright, can make reasonable movements and stay balanced. You can also make 2D Plasticine figures which lie flat on painted backdrops (see *Flat 2D animation* on page 148).

Other stop motion

Almost anything can be used to make stop motion – whiteboards, coloured paper cutouts, toys, furniture, plants, artwork and even people.

Search Google or YouTube for *'stop motion'* and you'll see some very innovative examples of what other people have done. In the picture below a group of children are driving around the room on chairs while the blocks on the table are forming words.

In the second example, the goodies are chasing the baddies. Note the body posture and the alignment of the guns.

This example used colour paper cutouts. Some parts are glued together. Other parts are not attached and can be animated.

In this last example, colourful cushions were placed on the floor and moved like a puzzle to solve the pattern.

What equipment do I need?

To make stop motion you'll need:
- Computer (this book uses Mac OS software, although the tasks can easily be applied to other computer platforms such as PC or iPad)
- GarageBand audio recording software
- iStopMotion software
- iMovie editing software
- Microphone
- Camera and cable (USB or Firewire), or
  an iPad, iPhone or iPod Touch with a camera (called a remote camera)
- Camera tripod, mount or stand
- Characters, eg LEGO®, Plasticine etc
- A sturdy table or surface (or portable stage)
- Backgrounds, eg large sheets of cardboard
- Props
- Art supplies to decorate props and backgrounds – paint, coloured paper
- Lights.

File names

In the process of making a stop motion you'll need to create a large number of files on your computer:
- GarageBand file – the soundtrack
- Soundtrack audio file exported from GarageBand (.aif or .aiff)
- iStopMotion file – the pictures (.mov format)
- iMovie project file (iMovie stores this within the iMovie Library)
- Final movie with title and credits exported from iMovie (MP4 format).

It is easier and tidier if you have a file storage and naming system that clearly identifies all the files associated with the project:

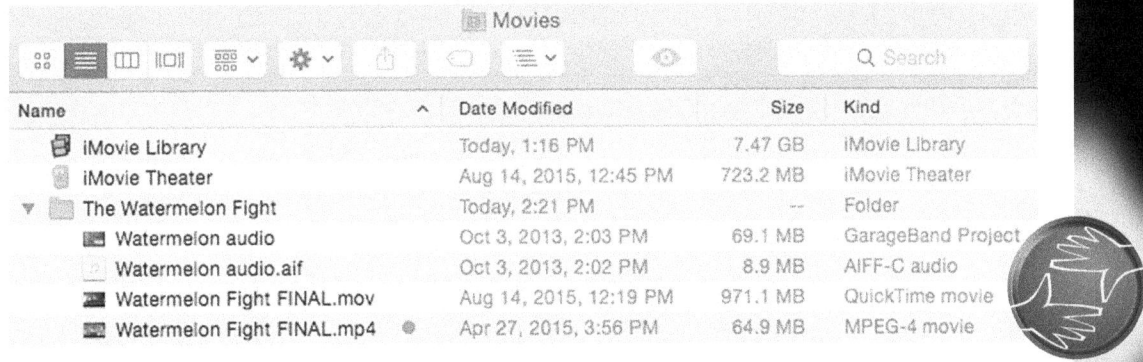

- Create a folder in the Movies folder for the stop motion project
- Give each file a descriptive name and use file suffixes for clarity
- The iStopMotion file appears as a QuickTime movie. To open this file in iStopMotion (eg to add more pictures) right-click and select 'Open with iStopMotion'. Double-clicking this file will open it in QuickTime Player. This is a large file size because it contains uncompressed pictures. The final movie file is much smaller because the pictures are compressed into a movie stream
- Add the word FINAL to the final version and colour it red. This is the file to upload to the internet (marked with red tag).

Aug(De)Mented Reality
by Hombre McSteez

Using a unique animation technique involving traditional animation cels, Hombre McSteez turns everyday life into a creature infested cartoon universe.
www.youtube.com/watch?v=gpum4nK2wOM

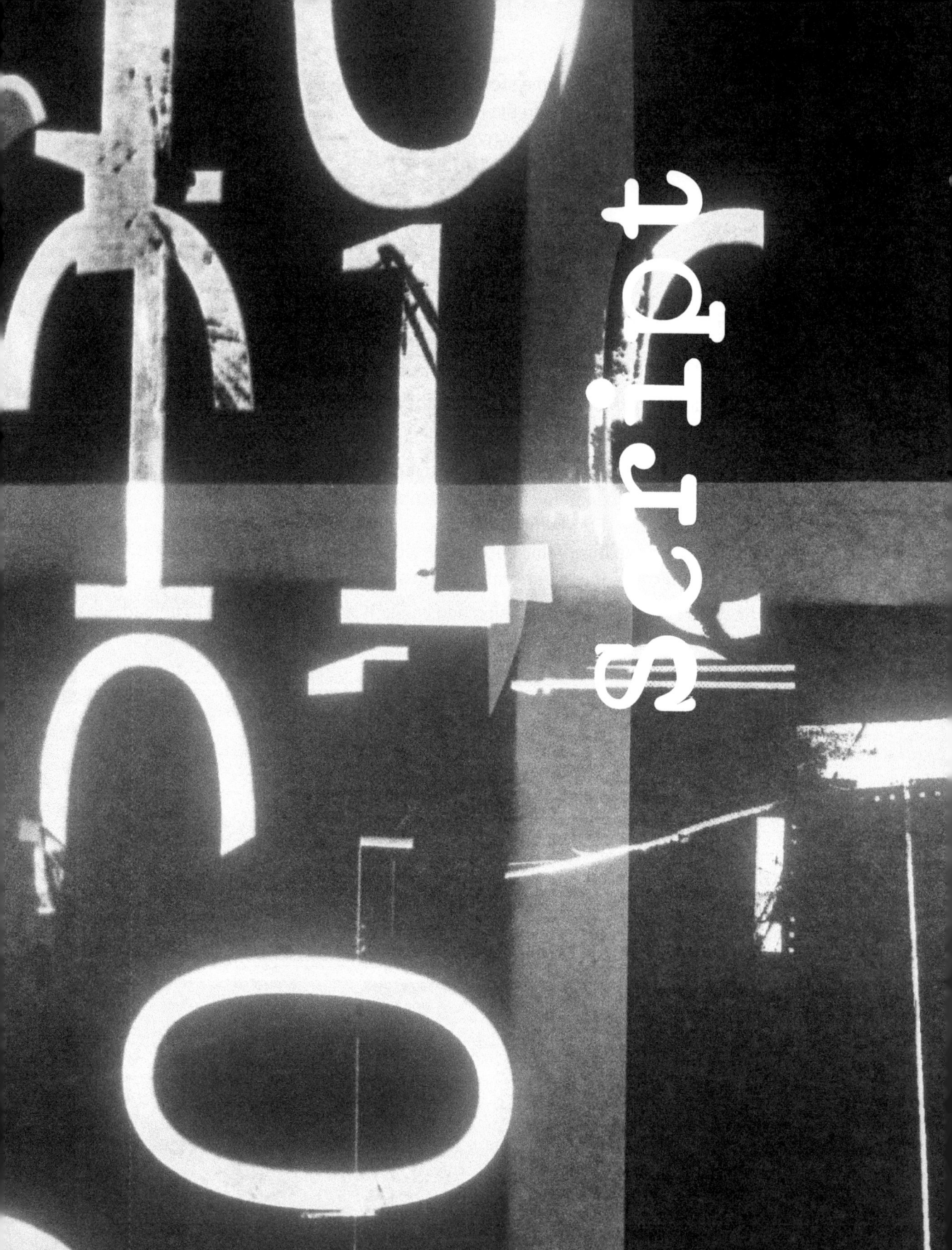

Script

When learning about stop motion, it seems inevitable that most people will jump straight into opening the iStopMotion software and making a start recording pictures. It is a great way to learn, but there comes a time when you, and your audience, have reached the limit of watching movies about chairs moving around the room. At this point it is time to go back a step and start your movie with a story.

There are a number of levels of story development:

- Simple processes, eg a paper dart being folded or a 'fly on the wall' view of a room being set up for an event
- A message but not necessarily a story, eg TV advertisements (see page 31)
- Stories with a plot (see page 18).

Even if your movie is a music video, you'll need to tell a story so it is not just a series of random activities.

In this chapter you will learn how to write the script for your stop motion.

What makes a great movie?

Think about a favourite movie:

- What did you like about it?
- Summarise the story in one sentence.

Now think about a movie you didn't like:

- Why didn't you like it?

You'll probably find that the key to a good movie is a good story rather than special effects.

> A **story** is the main event that takes place. It should fit on one page.
>
> A **script** is the specific detail of who says or does what. It will be many pages depending on the length of the movie.

It is possible to tell a great story really badly, or to boring story brilliantly (the second of these may be more watchable). Aim for a good story told through a good script.

Some people say that in all the world there are only six stories. All other stories are in some way a variation of these core stories. This is why we see a lot of similarities between the stories in different movies, eg in *Lion King* and *Madagascar 2* (and others), a son wants to please his father but instead causes a disaster and runs away. After some soul searching he comes back home to seek restoration and succeeds.

Even if your movie is mostly about a battle, take the time to develop a story to explain the battle or action sequence:

- What is at stake?
- Who is on each side, and why?
- What happens if the battle is won?
- What happens if the battle is lost?

And don't forget about humour. Look out for little moments which give the audience a smile. You don't need to turn every movie into a comedy, but when recording the audio you may want to keep a word slip up or ad lib. Look out for areas where the choice of props can add interest, or a character movement can add personality. It could simply be pausing between action and response allowing the audience time to ponder what is going to happen.

Different types of stories – genres

The genre is the general style of how the story is told. Every story fits into one genre or another, or sometimes they are a combination of several genres. Familiarise yourself with the 'rules' for your genre.

The same story told in the style of different genres will result in completely different movies, even though the characters and events in the story are the same.

Here are some of the basic rules for popular genres (search *'movie genre'* for more information):

- **Action** – high energy movies, stunts, chases, rescues, battles. Often two dimensional – good guy/bad guy. Includes movies about an outlaw fighting for justice or battling a tyrant (*Robin Hood, Zorro* or *Star Wars*), pirates (*Pirates of the Caribbean, Hook*) or searching for a lost city or for hidden treasure (*Indiana Jones*)

- **Comedy** – light hearted plots deliberately designed to amuse and provoke laughter by exaggerating every aspect of the story. Includes movies such as *Zoolander, Monsters Inc., Home Alone* and *The Princess Bride*

- **Drama** – serious life stories with realistic situations and characters. Not focused on special effects, comedy or action. Includes movies such as *Miss Potter, Saving Mr Banks* and *Finding Neverland*

- **Horror** – includes a hero who has a flaw and a fear. Your 'monster' needs to be truly evil, and you need to include several 'false alarms' to increase tension. You also need to isolate your hero so that they have no escape from the monster. At the end, suggest that the monster is not really gone. Horror movies include the stop motion *Coraline*

- **Romance** – any movie in which the story revolves around the romantic involvement of the hero/ine who needs to make decisions based on a newly-found romantic attraction. The appeal of these movies is in the dramatic reality of the emotions expressed by the characters. The story needs a happy ending (or at least bittersweet). Movies include *Titanic, Pride and Prejudice* and *High School Musical*

- **Spy** – when a villain tries to obtain secret information, a spy is assigned to stop them. Spy movies often feature secret headquarters, an agent known by a number and a beautiful foreign agent who becomes the love of the hero. Popular in movies like *Spy Kids, Johnny English, Cats & Dogs, James Bond* and *Austin Powers*.

There are possibly hundreds of genres and popular trends often create new ones. Here are some more: Adventure, Alien, Animal, Animation, Chick Flick, Crime, Disaster, Documentary, Epic, Family, Fantasy, Film-noir, Mockumentary, Musical, Mystery, Science Fiction, Sequel, Silent, Sport, Thriller, War, Western.

Developing the story

There are many ways to create a story for stop motion including writing, adapting and improvising. Here is an overview of the stages of development for each method:

	Write a script	Adapt a story	Improvise a story
Ideas	✔		✔
Writing	✔		
Editing	✔	✔	
Recording audio	✔	✔	✔

In general, shorter stories work best. You need to find the core story and omit information that is not important to the story, or that can be shown another way. Remember that every second of soundtrack needs to be animated. So if in doubt, make it shorter.

Writing a script

This is a bit like writing an essay, but the result is a movie script. If you want an original movie you'll need a script crafted from the essence of a unique story. Go to *Writing a script* on page 19.

Adapting a story for a script

Written stories can be a good start, but they need to be adapted for a movie.

If you've ever read a book and then watched the movie version you'll know that it might take ten hours to read the book, but only 2 hours to watch the movie. The movie aims to tell the main essence of the story. A lot of the story has either been conveyed in another way, or has been omitted. Go to *Adapting a story for a script* on page 24.

Improvising a script

A quick, fun and collaborative way to create a story is improvisation. This method is great for group work because everyone gets to take part in creating the soundtrack.

Don't write anything down. Don't try to plan ahead. Just answer the story outline questions one at a time and you'll create an original story.

Go to *Improvising a script* on page 26.

Writing a script

Here is an overview of the process to write a script for your stop motion movie.

Step 1: Writing a premise

A story needs to be about something. That something is the premise. It's the central idea and the reason people want to watch the movie. It's often an open question: **'What might happen if...?'**

> ### Movie premises
>
> *Bee Movie (2007) – what might happen if bees find out that humans are taking their honey?*
>
> *High School Musical (2006) – what might happen if someone follows their own dreams instead of dreams other people have for them?*
>
> *Monsters Inc. (2001) – what might happen if children stop being scared of monsters?*
>
> *Toy Story 1 (1995) – what might happen if toys come to life when their owner is out of the room?*
>
> *Groundhog Day (1993) – what might happen if you live the same day over and over again and have the chance to change your choices?*

A good premise should be:

- brief – ideally one sentence (maximum 25 words)
- an idea that jumps out at you
- in the present tense.

Sometimes people waste a lot of time trying to improve a story that's not worth telling because the premise is not interesting.

Step 2: Questions which develop the premise

Use techniques like brainstorming or mind maps to get good ideas that develop your premise.

Suppose your premise is 'What might happen if I wake up one morning and find I can fly?'

What questions come to mind?
- Where will I fly to?
- How fast can I fly?
- What can I do that is better than walking?
- In what way is flying more risky than walking?
- How could I use this ability for my own advantage?
- How would I use this ability to benefit others?
- How long will this ability last – just one day, from now on, or until I make a mistake?
- Would I be the same size as I am now, or shrunk to the size of a bird?
- Do I fly with my arms, or have I grown wings?
- Would I still go to school?
- What would my parents think?
- What would my friends think?
- What would be my greatest goal with my ability to fly?
- What would be my greatest barrier to achieving this goal?

Your answers to these questions may lead you to a particular idea which could become your story.

Alternatively, these answers may help you define a character which you can write into an existing story. For example, come up with your own original version of *'The three little (flying) pigs'*.

The next step is to take all those ideas you've come up with and combine the best of them into a story.

Step 3: Writing the story outline

A story outline connects the various separate ideas you want in the story. One good way to develop a story outline is to use small plot cards. On each card write one event, important action or key line of dialogue. Use as many cards as you need to tell the whole story.

Place the cards down on a table in a line and read through the story:
- Does the story flow?
- What happens if you move a card to a different order?
- Do you need to add scenes on extra cards?
- Do each of the main characters have a significant role?

> *Trey Parker and Matt Stone, creators of South Park, share this tip for developing a story outline. If every point in a story outline can be connected to the next point with 'and then', the story seems to have no point. Whereas, if every point in the story is connected to the next point with 'but' or 'therefore', you have an engaging story.*
>
> *Emma Coats, a Pixar story artist, suggests this structure for the outline of a story: "Once upon a time there was ___. Every day, ___. One day ___. Because of that, ___. Because of that, ___. Until finally ___."*

When you are happy with the way your story develops, number each card so they don't get out of order.

Writing the story in three parts

Here is a common format for a dramatic story which is told in three parts (also called 'acts'):

- The **first part** introduces the hero of the story, the problem and also the villain
- The **second part** moves the heroine into the heart of the problem. By the end of the second act they are at a point when all hope seems lost
- The **third and final part** has a final confrontation and resolution of the problem.

If the pace of the story was drawn as a line it would look like this:

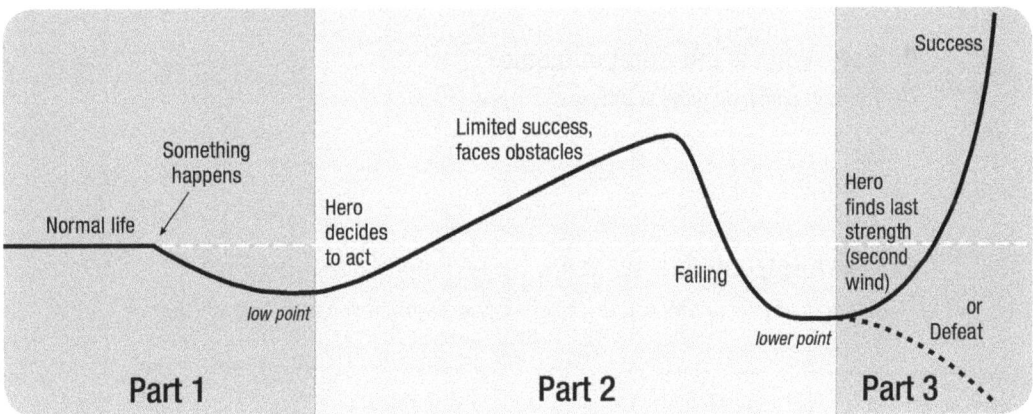

Use the table on the next page to help write the story outline in 3-parts (download a copy of the story outline at *stop-motion-handbook.com/downloads.html*).

Story Outline

Write at least one sentence for each of these seven questions.

Part 1

Opening scene – Where are you? What are you doing?
Defines the movie's time, place, theme and tone

Cause incident – What happens?
The event that sets the plot in motion

First turning point – What do you do about it?
The event that sets the hero on their journey

Part 2

Confrontation and conflict – What stops you?
The heroine forges ahead on the mission but faces obstacles

Defeat – What is the worst outcome?
The point at which all hope seems lost

Part 3

Second turning point – What is your last chance for success?
The life or death event that will test the hero's strength, resolve and moral courage

Resolution – What is the final outcome?
The payoff in which the heroine either triumphs or sacrifices themselves for the greater good

stop-motion-handbook.com/downloads.html

Step 4: Writing the story into a script

Take your story outline and add details to bring the story to life. Determine which characters you need and write the lines of dialogue. List the artwork/props required. Make notes about actions and scene changes – you don't want a movie that is non-stop talking without a break.

> It can be easier to record dramatic or 'acted' voices if people don't need to concentrate on reading. A script can be written as a sequence of points so the actual words are improvised when recorded.
>
> Or you could take the story outline and improvise the dialogue without writing anything further.
>
> See *Improvising a script* on page 26.

Make the opening interesting or exciting to catch the audience's attention.

Leave spaces in the script for characters and the audience to ponder the seriousness of the situation, and to increase the tension, before the hero makes their move.

Read through the script. Is the story clear and does it have the right pace?

Make some connection between the start and the end, eg an unused object or idea from the start becomes useful in the resolution of the problem.

Labelling the scenes (optional)

Add labels to your script every time the location or time changes. Scene labels might indicate when you need to move the camera position or change the background. Labels in a movie script are different to chapter headings in a book because they describe the location rather than the action. It is conventional to use capital letters.

> When your story is written, go to *Creating a soundtrack* on page 40.

For more information on creating strong stories and developing compelling scripts refer to these resources:

- *Screenplay: The foundations of screenwriting* by Syd Field
- *Story: Substance, structure, style and the principles of screenwriting* by Robert McKee
- International Central Institute for Youth and Educational Television (IZI) *www.izi.de.*

Adapting a story for a script

Existing stories can be a good start for a script, but the written version may need to be adapted for the screen.

The biggest task will be to reduce the amount of words to achieve a script of the right length. The script needs to tell the main essence of the story as required for the style of the chosen genre.

Some written work, such as poems may be suitable for a soundtrack and do not require adapting.

Written story	Adapted for stop motion
It was a dark and scary night. The wind rustled through the trees and gave a shiver to your bones. Somewhere around midnight, the faint cry of a distant wolf pierced the darkness. Suddenly there was a crash at the door. The sound echoed around the metal hut like a ricocheting bullet.	**Sound:** Wind sounds with distant wolf howl (3 seconds). Loud sound of crash on metal with echo (2 seconds). **Background:** Dark, indistinct shapes with vertical strokes representing tree trunks. A full moon casts a ghostly reflection across part of the background. On one side is a cut away view of a small metal hut. **Animation:** Show the whole background for 3 seconds. When the crashing sound starts, show a close up of the hut followed by a rapid sequence of parts of the hut.
I'd been waiting at the bus stop for almost an hour and not even one vehicle had passed. It was the hottest day of summer and I was melting. I tried to think 'cool' thoughts like ice cream and soda, but that was just torture. Then an elephant turned up. "Hop on", it said.	**Sound:** Nature sounds such as crickets, or annoying 'elevator' type music (7 seconds, then a voice says "Hop on". **Background:** Street scene with bus stop. **Animation:** Show empty street. Character paces up and down street (3 seconds), looks at watch (close up for 1 second), character slumps to sit on ground (2 seconds). Large shadow moves over character (1 second). Character looks up and against the sun sees silhouette of elephant (2 seconds).

24

Characters need something to say unless you want a narrator to do all the talking.

Written story	Adapted for stop motion
Eva and Simon had never been to Mars before. They'd seen pictures of it, of course, but to actually be there was almost beyond words. "It's so beautiful", cried Eva.	**Narrator:** Eva and Simon had never been to Mars before. **Simon:** I'm speechless! **Eva:** It's so ... beautiful.
Quick pass me the guitar and I'll play you a song.	**Zebo:** Quick, pass me the guitar *(starts playing)*.

When your story is written and adapted for a movie, go to *Creating a soundtrack* on page 40.

Extreme Toys
by XTreme Video (Karim Rejeb)

Extreme sports stop motion with Playmobil characters on mountain bike and BMX.
www.youtube.com/watch?v=u3uPZZQVoCg

Improvising a script

Using a story outline just verbally answer the questions one at a time and you'll create an original story.

Here are some questions you can use to create a story in the 3-part format (see also *Story Outline* on page 22):

1) Where are you? (or what was your first thought this morning?)
2) What happens?
3) What do you do about it?
4) What stops you?
5) What is the worst outcome?
6) What is the last chance?
7) What is the final outcome?

These seven questions prompt the answers to create the next part of the story. Don't try to plan ahead. Don't write anything down. One question at a time, just decide the right voice tone for that part of the story and record the dialogue as it is improvised.

For the shortest soundtrack, answer each question with one sentence. You may end up with a movie that is around one minutes long. Or for a longer soundtrack use each question as a prompt to develop that part of the story.

If working with a group, it is not important to audition 'parts' as each person will answer their question from the perspective they feel makes sense. Several people can share the voice of one character.

We've developed longer story outlines (which have more questions) for different types of story genres such as alien, fairy and gangster. For more information go to *www.ipadanimation.net/store.html*

> When you are ready to record your improvised story, go to *Creating a soundtrack* on page 40.

Tips to develop a story

Watch and learn
You can learn how to write a good story by watching other people's movies – both good and bad. Watch all sorts of movies, not just stop motion ones, and not just your favourite type either.

The story must have a point
The story has to be about something or it will not capture the audience. A common plot is about someone whose life has been interrupted by an event or threat of an event. The story is about how they try to sort it out.

Movies are more successful if they have a good story rather than great special effects.

Choose a hero
Movies should have a hero/ine (also called a protagonist). The hero can be a group of people, an object or a place. They do not always have to be nice, but they should be intriguing.

Make your hero likeable and make their dilemmas something everyone can relate to. Many stories have a hero that the audience would like to be friends with.

Structure your story
Every story needs several parts – a beginning, a middle and an end.

When you have more confidence you can mix them up – start your story in the middle and follow it with the end. Then finish by telling the start of the story. For example, if you start your story with the ending, eg the villain knocks at the door, then tell rest of the story from the beginning so that we can see how the events led up to the villain knocking at the door.

Longer movies often have small side stories to help lead towards the one big story.

Avoid being linear
A story that starts at the very beginning and progresses through each event systematically may not be very exciting.

Don't tell the audience everything at once. Make your audience wonder what's going to happen next. But if you are going to reveal a mystery, make sure the outcome is worth waiting for.

Think about the ending first

In the movie *Titanic*, the director James Cameron ended the movie with an elderly lady who had been on the Titanic being reunited with a necklace she lost when the boat sank. He wrote the story about the Titanic from the point of view of that lady – starting when she was a young girl, the special occasion when she received the necklace and why she was on the boat.

Include a twist

The bigger the twist, the more the audience must feel they should have seen it coming. You need to plant ideas in the minds of your audience. You don't want to give the end away but the viewer should feel that the twist was, on reflection, inevitable and believable.

In *Madagascar – Escape 2 Africa*, a cranky old lady chases the lion at the start of the movie. She appears again chasing some penguins. When the movie is at its climax the old lady becomes the solution to the problem – to chase off the villain. The end is a surprise but also totally logical.

Stories and children

One of the most common themes in stories for children is transformation. The transformation is generally from less powerful to more powerful, or to more glamorous and magical.

Other common themes in stories for children include:
- *Triumph of good over evil*
- *Trickery*
- *Hero's quest*
- *Reversal of fortune*
- *Small outwitting the big (David and Goliath).*

Mattel once asked some children to make up a story about a superhero who had just captured the ultimate Dr. Evil.

They found out that the girls wanted to rehabilitate him, whereas, the boys told in gory detail how they'd do all sorts of horrendous things to finish the villain off.

Extract from *Wired* magazine Michael Meloan, quoting President of Mattel Media, Doug Glen in an interview on the differences between the ways girls and boys play.

Don't try to be too clever

Simple stories work best. Don't try to be too clever or complex.

Good stories often include true events from the writer's life. For example, if you love animals, you may be able to write a good story about someone who makes friends with wild animals or even dinosaurs.

Be original

Be true to yourself. Don't simply copy others. You may be tempted to use famous quotes or jokes from other people's movies – this might be OK when you are learning to make movies but try to come up with your own funny lines. Good movies stand out because they are unique.

Pixar's Rules of Storytelling

Emma Coats, *Pixar* story artist, has produced *Pixar's 22 Rules of Storytelling*. See the full list on *www.aerogrammestudio.com/2013/03/07/pixars-22-rules-of-storytelling*. Here are some of them:

- Simplify. Focus. Combine characters. Hop over detours. You'll feel like you're losing valuable stuff but it sets you free
- What is your character good at, comfortable with? Throw the opposite at them. Challenge them. How do they deal with it?
- When you're stuck, make a list of what wouldn't happen next. Lots of times the material to get you unstuck will show up
- Discount the 1st thing that comes to mind. And the 2nd, 3rd, 4th, 5th – get the obvious out of the way. Surprise yourself
- If you were your character, in this situation, how would you feel? Honesty lends credibility to unbelievable situations
- Coincidences to get characters into trouble are great; coincidences to get them out of it are cheating.

> ### Movie competitions
>
> *Some movie competitions give participants a number of elements that must be included in the movie such as a particular prop, character name, line of dialogue or genre. It can be fun trying to work out how to write a story that uses those elements in a clever way. It can also be very fast-paced because you've got a limited time to make it and a maximum movie length.*

Writing a TV advertisement

A fun stop motion project is to create a television advertisement. The script needs a very clear message – which could actually be a very short story.

Step 1: Write down the product or service you want to advertise

Step 2: Name three FEATURES

List three features or good points (facts) about the product or service, eg the wrapper is edible, the battery lasts for a month, it fits in your pocket.

Step 3: Name three BENEFITS to the customer, public or audience

For each feature write HOW the customer will benefit. The customer needs to be convinced that your product or service will save them money, be more convenient, be safer, smell better etc. They can be funny or serious, but have to be possible or believable.

Step 4: Write the advertisement

Using the benefits, write the script for a 30 second advertisement. If you are advertising a relaxing holiday you'll want to have a relaxed pace, so might only have time for 20 – 30 words. If it is a new 'must have, get in quick' thing, you'll probably talk faster and fit in 50 words.

Time yourself as you read the advertisement – 30 seconds is 30 seconds – not 32. Are there any wasted words you can remove?

Read your script to someone else. Do they feel you've convinced them to buy? Change what you've written if you need to.

Step 5: Make your stop motion advertisement

- Record your soundtrack (go to Creating a soundtrack on page 40)
- Make your character and props (see *Props and set up* chapter on page 73)
- Record your stop motion pictures (see *Pictures* chapter on page 107).

Audio

A note about music and copyright

Using music from your favourite band can make your movie really great. However, technically this is stealing. So while it is a good way to learn how to make movies, you won't be able to have them shown on TV or enter them in a movie competition unless you have obtained permission to use the music.

Sometimes it is worth asking the band because they just might say 'yes'! But it is usually easier, and quicker, to buy royalty free music from an online supplier for a small cost, or else make your own in GarageBand.

In this chapter you will record the soundtrack for your stop motion. You will learn about:

- The importance of high quality sound
- Equipment to record sound
- Using GarageBand
- Challenges with sound
- Tips for great sound
- Sound effects
- Saving your soundtrack.

Which of these do you think would make the biggest difference to the overall quality of your movie?

A) Using a better camera for a clearer picture? or

B) Using a better microphone for crisper sound?

In most cases, if the sound is clear, your audience will think the picture quality is better than it is. Whereas, if your sound is poor, even with the best quality pictures in the world, your audience may think the movie is low quality. So, **invest in better sound equipment and learn better recording techniques before you buy a better camera.**

Let's see how big the challenge of good quality sound is:

Shut your eyes and listen. How many different sounds can you hear?

What do you think you can do to achieve a quiet location for recording good sound? (see *Sound versus noise* on page 56).

Microphones

Here is a summary of the types of microphones to help you choose the best quality for stop motion:

- **Condenser** microphones are sensitive to loud sounds. They have a greater frequency response for low and high sounds, and produce a high quality sound. Condenser microphones are more expensive
- **Dynamic** microphones are cheaper and more robust. They have a limited frequency response so the sound quality is not as accurate.

Microphones are designed to record specific types of sound, called pick-up patterns:

- **Uni-directional, zoom** or **shotgun** microphones record sounds from a specific direction. These microphones should give the best quality audio recordings for stop motion soundtracks. The microphone pictured (*Sennheiser ME-66*) is held in a rubber mount which reduces the noise transmitted through the microphone stand
- **Omni-directional** microphones record sounds and noises from all directions. This is the type of microphone on most computers and cameras.

Microphones are available with either **USB connector**, 3-pin **XLR connector** or **3.5mm phono connector**.

- **USB** connectors produce digital sound and can be attached directly to a computer. Low quality microphones may have a slight delay called 'latency', but this should not be a problem in the way we suggest recording a soundtrack
- **XLR** connectors usually give a higher sound quality because they are 'balanced' and therefore not very susceptible to noise and interference. They cannot be directly plugged into a computer because the connector doesn't fit. However, they can be connected via a breakout box (see *Apogee* on next page)
- The **3.5mm phono** connector may require a special converter cable such as the *Griffin Microphone GarageBand Cable* because the sound signal in a microphone is different to normal audio. Microphones with these connectors are affordable but they are often 'unbalanced' and more susceptible to noise and interference.

Equipment to record sound

(in order of potential audio recording quality):

Connect a separate XLR microphone to your computer via a breakout box such as the Apogee Solo or Duet *(very high quality)*:

- High quality XLR microphones connect directly into this breakout box which connects to the USB port on the computer
- Record sound directly into GarageBand
- This method is like a recording studio and should be considered for serious stop motion work.

Connect a USB microphone to your computer *(high quality)*:

- High quality USB microphone (such as *Apogee MiC*) connects to the USB port on the computer. The *Logitech HD Pro C920 webcam* may be a logical choice as it can record sound, and later be used to record pictures
- Record sound directly into GarageBand.

Connect a separate microphone to the 3.5mm phono line-in port on your computer *(good quality, may need special cable)*:

- Record sound directly into GarageBand or iMovie
- You will need a special cable such as the *Griffin Microphone GarageBand Cable*.

Connect a separate microphone to a video camera *(good quality, longer 2 step process)*:

- Record sound into the camera as you would do for video
- Upload it to iMovie
- Edit the audio in iMovie or export to GarageBand.

Use the built-in microphone on your computer *(medium quality, easy, cheap)*:

- Record sound directly into GarageBand or iMovie
- Raise computer on high table so you can comfortably stand close to microphone.

Use the built-in microphone on a video camera *(medium quality, easy, cheap, longer 2 step process)*:

- Record sound into the camera as for video, and upload it to iMovie, or connect the camera to the computer and record the sound directly into GarageBand
- Edit the audio in iMovie, or export to GarageBand.

GarageBand

GarageBand is possibly the most misunderstood application on your computer. The reason is that if someone regards themselves as 'non-musical' they may come across images of instruments and decide that GarageBand is not for them.

Our goal in this chapter is to give everyone confidence using GarageBand for creating a soundtrack for a stop motion. This software is a vital tool for making stop motion regardless of any interest or ability in music.

These notes are only an introduction to the vast possibilities of GarageBand. For more information refer to GarageBand's help guides and tutorials or go to *www.apple.com/mac/garageband*.

GarageBand is specifically designed to create multi-layered sounds for music and soundtracks. It is like an orchestra in a box, and then much more. To get the full potential from GarageBand you probably need some musical knowledge, but there are many versatile features for beginners. There are controls to refine the sound to produce an endless number of unique possibilities. Experiment with the controls until you get the perfect sound.

GarageBand soundtracks can include audio from a wide range of sources such as:

- voice and dialogue recorded with a microphone
- music and sound effects recorded with a microphone
- actual music notes (MIDI) recorded from a real instrument such as a keyboard or guitar with a USB output or GarageBand's in-built keyboard
- loops
- sound effect files
- iTunes music and MP3s
- audio from Quicktime movies.

GarageBand is capable of producing high quality sounds. To make a proper assessment of the quality of your soundtrack, you will need to listen to it through quality speakers – not little computer speakers. This may mean connecting the sound from your computer to your home stereo. A second best option is to plug headphones into your computer. This is particularly important if your movie will be seen on an iPad or a home theatre system.

The GarageBand window

Let's start off with a quick overview of the names of various parts of the GarageBand screen.

Open GarageBand. If you are presented with the option for a new project select 'Voice'.

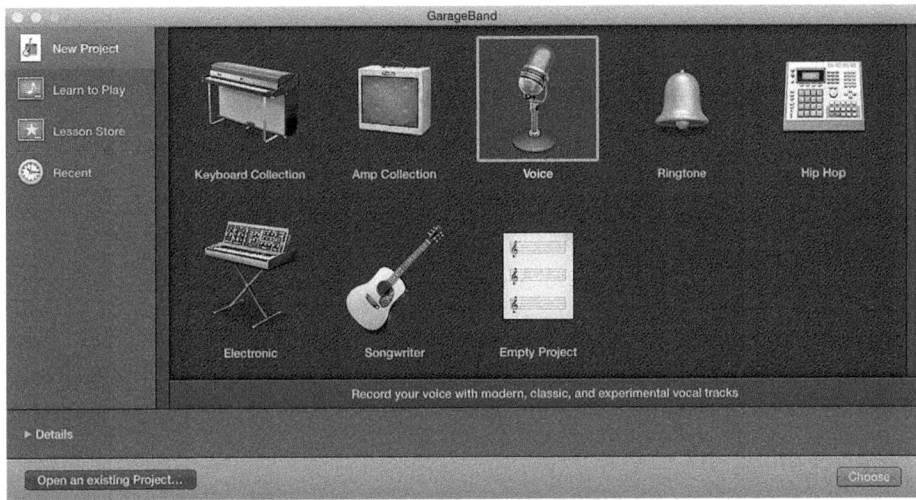

The GarageBand window has a number of parts. Not all of them may be displayed when you open a new project, but we will use them all in creating the soundtrack.

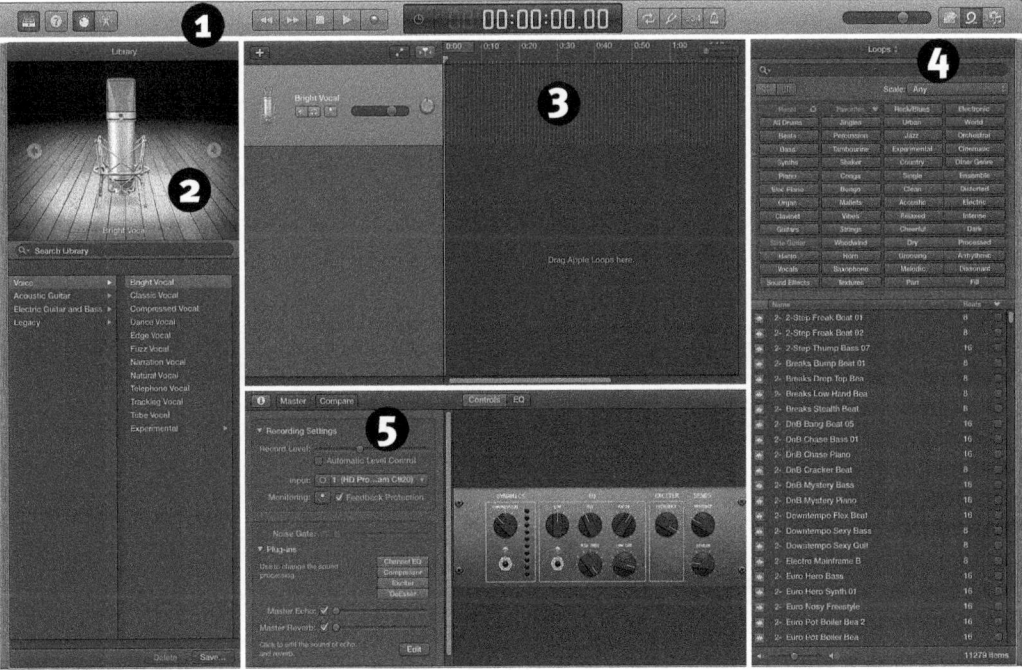

❶ Control bar

Across the top of the GarageBand window the Control bar has buttons for customising the display.

LCD Display

The LCD Display in the centre of the Control bar gives information about the soundtrack. Click the icon at the left end to switch the display mode from 'Beats' to 'Time' to show seconds and minutes.

❷ Library

The left of the window can show the Library which contains instruments and patches used for selecting the type of sound in each Track in the Workspace. The Library button (Y) in the Control bar hides or shows the Library.

❸ Workspace

The Workspace is the main area where you record and edit the various audio clips of dialogue, music, loops and sound effects. Audio clips are stored in Tracks. The Track header has a picture showing the type of sound in that track as well as the volume.

Across the top of the Workspace, the Ruler marks the time and has a (small down-pointing triangle) which moves along it to show the part of the soundtrack being played. The window scrolls from right to left as the music plays.

The right end of the Ruler has a Horizontal Zoom control to adjust the magnification of the Workspace tracks.

❹ Loop/Media Browser

The right of the window can show browsers for selecting pre-recorded content such as loops and music. The Loop Browser button (O) and the Media Browser button (F) in the Control bar ❶ hide or show the browsers.

❺ Smart Controls and Editor

The bottom of the window is for Smart Controls 👣 (B) and Editors ✂ (E) to modify the sound in the track.

Smart Controls include an Inspector ⓘ for setting the Record Level and adding effect plug-ins.

There are different Editors for different types of instruments. For creating a soundtrack we'll use the Editor for a magnified view of the audio clip waveforms.

More information will be given about Smart Controls and the Editor as required in the task of creating a soundtrack.

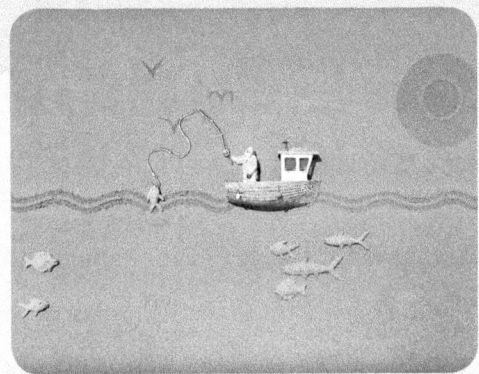

Gulp. Largest stop motion
by Sumo Science and Aardman for Nokia

A short film depicting a fisherman going about his daily catch. World record for the 'largest stop-motion animation set'. Recorded from a crane high over a beach
www.youtube.com/watch?v=ieN2vhslTTU

Gulp. The making of.

Creating a soundtrack

To prepare for a soundtrack it's best to simplify the GarageBand window:

- Delete extra audio tracks – select the Track header and CMD-Delete. It doesn't matter which track you keep but 'Bright Vocal' is a good choice to start with and it can be changed during editing
- Save the file with an appropriate name - File⟶Save.

Prepare for recording with a microphone (see *Recording with a microphone* on page 51). In particular, you'll need to:

- Set the Input source (microphone) on the Inspector ⓘ
- Set the number of channels (mono or stereo) on the Inspector
- Test and set Record Level on the Inspector
- Turn off Metronome 🔔 and Count-in 1234 in the Control bar.

Ensure you have the best recording conditions (see *Sound versus noise* on page 56 and *Tips for great sound* on page 57).

There are many types of stop motion project. These steps follow a useful process for recording a dialogue driven soundtrack.

40

Step 1: Recording the dialogue

Start by recording all the lines of dialogue:

1) **Record voices individually** – The best way to record dialogue is to use one track for each character voice. This takes more time, but recording each voice individually allows you to get the best recording of each person and therefore the best overall recording. It is easy to adjust the timing between each audio clip. The volume can be changed for each track or an effect applied to a track.

2) **Record character voices together** – If you are working with people who have good voice projection, have practised the script and are all likely to give their best performance at the same time, it is very easy to have everyone stand around the microphone and record them together. This can be a quick process, but it is harder to fix things later, such as making one voice louder or adjusting the timing between lines.

There are two approaches to recording dialogue:

1) **Record into one track** – Record each audio clip along the first track. Before each recording, make sure the Playhead is after the previous clip.

2) **Record into multiple tracks** – Each clip is named according to the name of the track it was recorded into. So for the easiest editing, create and name a track for each character. CTRL-click a header to add a new Audio Track – then CTRL-click the Track header to rename it as the name of the character.

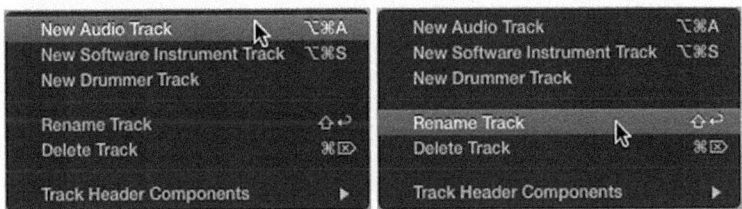

Before each recording, select the appropriate Track header and make sure the Playhead is after the previous clip.

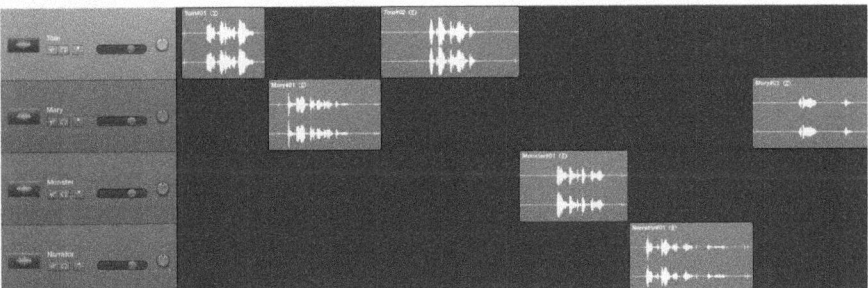

Sound recording process

Recording high quality sound is an important part of a stop motion movie. Follow this process to record with a microphone:

- Select the Track header *(highlights in light grey)*, and move the Ruler Playhead to the position you want to record
- Say *"Quiet on set"* so everyone in the room knows to be quiet
- Press R or click the red Record button
- Wait two seconds to record silence at the start – *this will make it easier to edit later*
- Speak clearly and expressively
- Wait two seconds to record silence at the end
- If you think you can improve *(make your words clearer or put more expression into your voice)*, have another go, otherwise
- Press the spacebar or click the Stop button.

If your sound is crisp and clear your audience will think the pictures are better than they are.

If your sound is poor, even the best pictures in the world won't stop your audience thinking the movie is low quality.

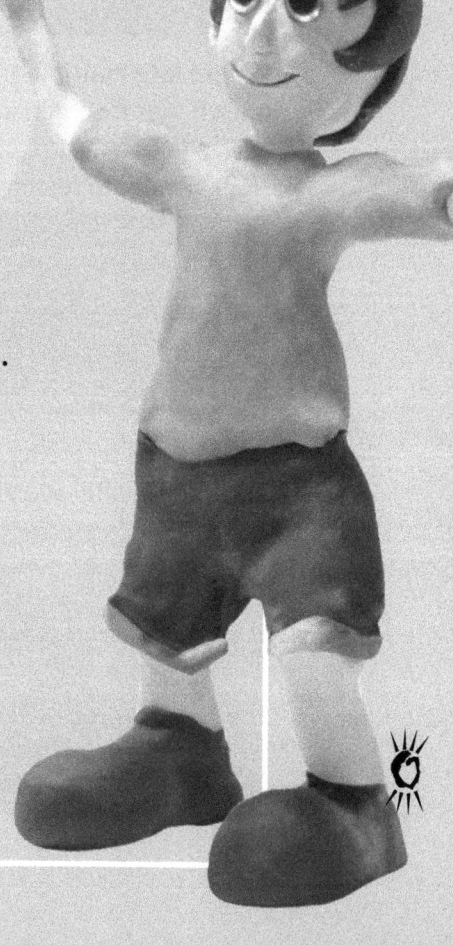

> *Voice Auditions*
>
> *Match the right voice to the character. Have each person test each character voice and agree the best fit. Ask other people to be voice talent if necessary.*

Repeat the Sound recording process (see opposite page) to record all dialogue.

After all dialogue is recorded:

- Listen to each clip and assess the quality of the recording: Is the volume too loud or soft? Is the voice tone appropriate? Are there unwanted noises? Record it again if you need to
- Identify the best take for each clip and trim unwanted recording and noise (see *Editing the soundtrack* on page 68).

Step 2: Reviewing the dialogue timing

Drag the centre of the first clip along the first track (move other clips out of the way if necessary) so the dialogue starts after the title. Allow 5 seconds at the start for a short stop motion or 10 seconds for a longer stop motion.

Starting from the left, drag the centre of each audio clip along their respective tracks so they play at the right time with all other parts of the dialogue and the soundtrack flows. Add tracks if necessary to assist with the arrangement of clips that need to play at the same time.

Assess the flow of the soundtrack and the timing between the lines of dialogue by miming the actions. An unbroken stream of talking can be exhausting to watch, so add small gaps to allow the story to breathe and consider the following:

- Does the flow of conversation sound natural, or are the spaces between lines of dialogue too short or too long?
- Are there extra spaces to allow characters to think, plot, react?
- Are there spaces to allow for travel or transitions between scenes or chases?
- Are there spaces between key scenes for music and visual panoramas?
- Is there a space for the title to be displayed? (see *Audio for title and credits* on page 46).

Remember that every second of soundtrack requires animation pictures. So if in doubt, make spaces shorter.

A soundtrack can be enhanced by changing the sound of audio clips (see *Apply effects* on page 46).

Step 3: Adding sound effects

The quickest way to add a sound effect may be to record your own with a microphone. So if you need a door slam, ticking clock, fingernail scraping across a board or someone snoring, use the same method for recording dialogue:

- Add a new Audio track
- Temporarily place the Playhead after the end of the last audio clip in the Workspace
- Record the sound (see *Sound recording process* on page 42)
- Trim the audio clip and slide it along the track to the right place.

Garageband has hundreds of sound effects as loops (see *Adding loops* on page 65).

Garageband also has other sound effects which are accessed by creating a track for a keyboard instrument. From the Library 📇 (Y) select the Legacy⟶Garageband⟶Sound Effects patch and then play a note on the musical keyboard (Window⟶Keyboard).

Another way to get sound effects is to search for *'royalty free sound effects'* or *'free sound effects'* and add them to iTunes (see *Adding other media* on page 60).

You can add several sound effects into the same track.

Step 4: Adding ambience sounds

Ambience sounds (also called atmosphere or soundscape) are generally very quiet and used to convey that the movie scene is taking place in a particular location such as a park, cafe, school, factory or laboratory. They may play for an entire scene or the start of a scene. Ambience sounds are a good way of disguising noise in the dialogue recording.

Follow the instructions in Step 3 above to either record your own or search for *'royalty free ambience sound'* or *'free ambience sound'*.

Garageband has a number of soundscapes which are accessed by creating a track for a keyboard instrument. From the Library 📇 (Y) select the Synthesizer⟶Soundscape patch and then play a note on the musical keyboard (Window⟶Keyboard).

Step 5: Adding music

Movies are powerful when the pictures and sound work together:

- Music can transform dialogue recordings from 'normal everyday talking' to something 'epic'
- Music is often the first thing heard in a stop motion and functions as a theme tune
- Music conveys a lot about the tone of the story, and a change of tone, so it is important to choose appropriate music

- Music brings continuity to changing picture angles of the same scene
- Music is a good way of disguising noise in the dialogue recording.

Music files and MP3s can be added. Search *'royalty free music'* or *'free music for video'* (see *Adding other media* on page 60):

- Click the Media Browser button 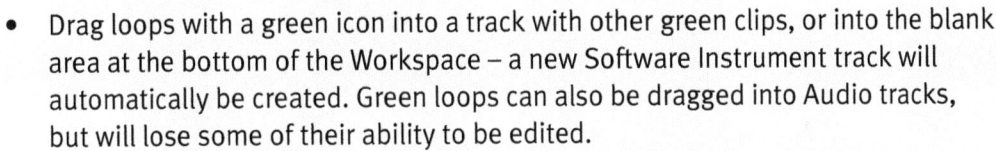 (F) and search for the required music file
- Drag the music file into the appropriate place in an Audio track or into the blank area at the bottom of the Workspace – a new Audio track will automatically be created. You can also drag files directly from the desktop into the GarageBand window without using the Media Browser.

Loops – short repeating tunes. GarageBand comes with thousands of loops (see *Adding loops* on page 65):

- Click the Loop Browser button 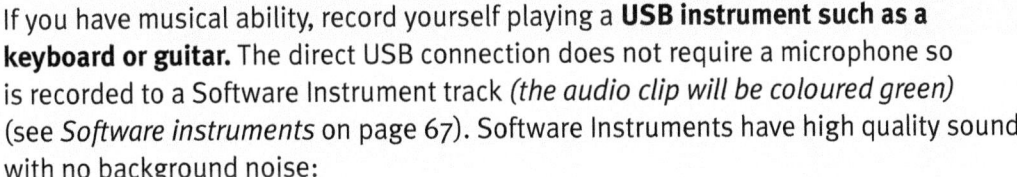 (O) and search for the required loops
- Drag loops with a blue icon to the appropriate place in an Audio track or into the blank area at the bottom of the Workspace – *a new Audio track will automatically be created*
- Drag loops with a green icon into a track with other green clips, or into the blank area at the bottom of the Workspace – a new Software Instrument track will automatically be created. Green loops can also be dragged into Audio tracks, but will lose some of their ability to be edited.

If you have musical ability, record yourself playing a **USB instrument such as a keyboard or guitar.** The direct USB connection does not require a microphone so is recorded to a Software Instrument track *(the audio clip will be coloured green)* (see *Software instruments* on page 67). Software Instruments have high quality sound with no background noise:

- Connect a USB musical instrument
- Click the New Track button ➕ and add a keyboard or guitar track
- From the Library 🖴 (Y) select the appropriate settings for the instrument you want. After the music is recorded, you can change the settings so the music is played by another instrument, eg trumpet or drums *(instruction on creating music with instruments is beyond the scope of this book)*.

Audio for title and credits

The movie title usually appears at the start of the movie. It could also appear after a few seconds of scenery, or after the first scene. The decision on where the title and credits are included in the movie, and how long they will be, often needs to be made at the time of creating the soundtrack in GarageBand so there is appropriate music, and a break in the dialogue:

- Allow at least five seconds of music for the title (see *Title* on page 121).
- Allow at least ten seconds of music for the credits (see *Credits* on page 123).

Step 6: Adjust the volume

At this point, the content of the soundtrack is complete. There are a couple of further steps to enhance the overall sound – the first of these is volume. The main goal is to ensure that dialogue can be clearly heard over other sounds, and that the soundtrack is balanced and comfortable to listen to.

The volume of each track can be adjusted with the volume slider in the Track header.

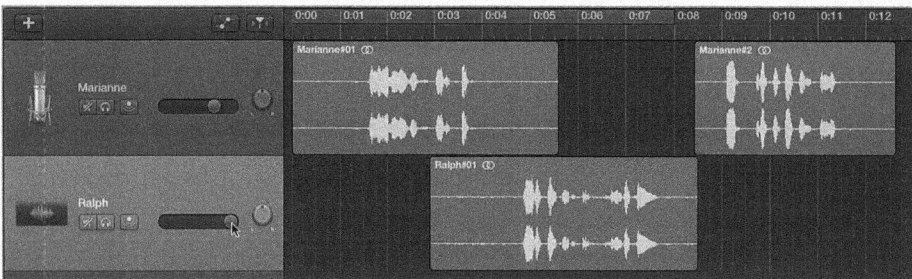

Within each track the volume can be adjusted for specific parts:

- Click the Automation button above the top Track header to reveal the volume line on each track
- Click the yellow line to add control points where you want to change the volume
- Drag points up to make the volume louder or down to make it quieter. This is a good way to ease in and out of clips without an abrupt edit point.

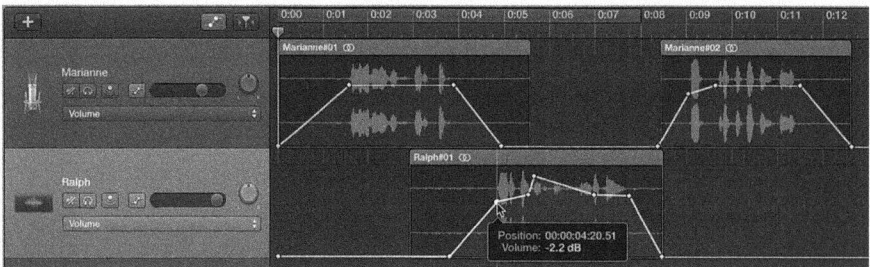

Step 7: Apply effects

When we recorded the dialogue, we used a track called 'Bright Voice'. Now is the time to review this, if required. Effects can change the dynamics of the sound, for example:

- If the story has some dialogue in a cave, and other dialogue in a house, they should sound different. The cave voice should have echoes
- If the same person voices the character of a child and an adult they should sound different. The pitch of the adult voice should be lower.

These above examples, and many more, are achieved through plug-in effects:

- Select the header of the track you want to change
- Click the Solo button 🎧 for that track, so only that track is heard
- From the Library 📇 (Y) select the Voice category
- Play the soundtrack and then click the Voice patches to hear the result. Garageband has other voice patches in the category Legacy⇢Garageband⇢Vocals.

If the patch produces the right sound, great! Repeat this process for each track.

Otherwise choose the patch that is closest to the sound you want and you can enhance it further with Smart Control Plug-ins to improve or customise the sound:

- Click the Smart Controls button 🐾 (B)
- Click the Inspector button 𝒊 and scroll to the bottom to see the Plug-in effects which have been applied to create the sound patch.

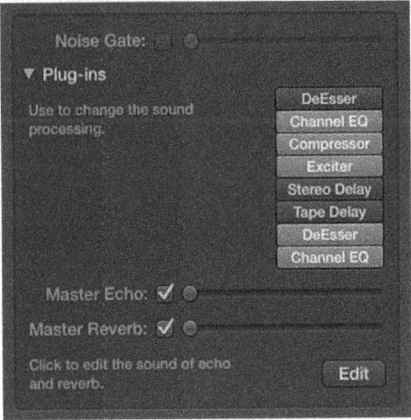

Plug-in effects make specific changes to the sound. Combining several Plug-ins give vast control over creating a unique sound.

Play the sound and click the left end of an effect name to turn it off and hear how sound changes.

Click the right end of the name to change this effect to another one.

Click the middle of the effect name to view and change the settings. Remember to play the sound and hear the result of the changes as you make them.

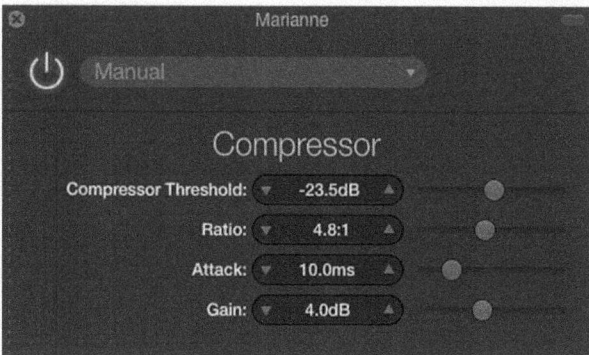

Each of the settings will change the overall sound effect, or you can click the name at the top of the effect settings and select one of the preset options.

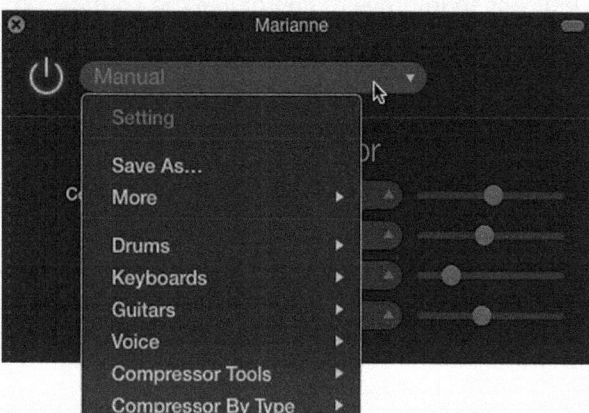

Some of the Plug-in effects can also be adjusted on the visual panel of knobs and switches.

Detailed explanation of plug-ins is beyond the scope of this book, but here is an explanation of some useful starter Plug-in effects:

- **Dynamics⇢Compressor**. A compressor adjusts the volume to smooth out sudden changes. Compressors can add punch and definition and make it sound better when played through small speakers or poor quality speakers.

  Threshold is the volume at which the Compressor changes the sound. Ratio is the amount of compression. Attack is the speed that the compression starts. If these settings reduce the volume of the sound, it can be increased with Gain

- **Dynamics⇢Noise Gate** (activates Noise Gate slider above Plug-ins panel). Reduces low-level noise by cutting off the sound when it falls below a certain level. Slide the Threshold as far right as possible to remove noise, but retain dialogue

- **Pitch⇢Pitch Shifter** changes the pitch of the dialogue without changing the speed. Set the Mix to 100% to hear the full effect

- **Reverb⇢Space Designer**. Reverb simulates the natural reflections of a sound in a surrounding space, eg the type of room or location will change the sound. Space Designer has a range of room types as diverse as a *Botta Church* or *Villa Bathroom*.

- **Audio Units⇢Apple⇢AULowPass**. Removes high pitch noise.

If you want to use the Combination of Plug-in effects on other tracks select Track⇢New Track with Duplicate Settings.

Step 8: Finalising the soundtrack

At this point the soundtrack should be complete. As a final check, play it and think about how it will work with the animation:

- Is there enough music at the start for the title? *If not, select all clips and move them along the track. Extend the music at the start*
- Is there enough time for the actions between parts of dialogue? *If not, move the relevant clips along the track*
- Is the dialogue easy to hear above the sound effects and music? *If not, adjust the track volume*
- Is there enough music at the end for the credits? *If not, extend the music at the end.*

Step 9: Saving the soundtrack

- Always save the GarageBand file – File→Save (**this is your master – don't lose it!**)
- Also to save the soundtrack as an audio file for use in another application, such as iStopMotion or iMovie, select Share→Export Song to Disk. The Share menu gives options for saving your soundtrack. The options vary slightly depending on whether your GarageBand file is a song or movie

- Select high quality AAC (saved with .m4a suffix) or MP3, or AIFF (uncompressed). Leave compression (to reduce the file size) until the movie is complete.

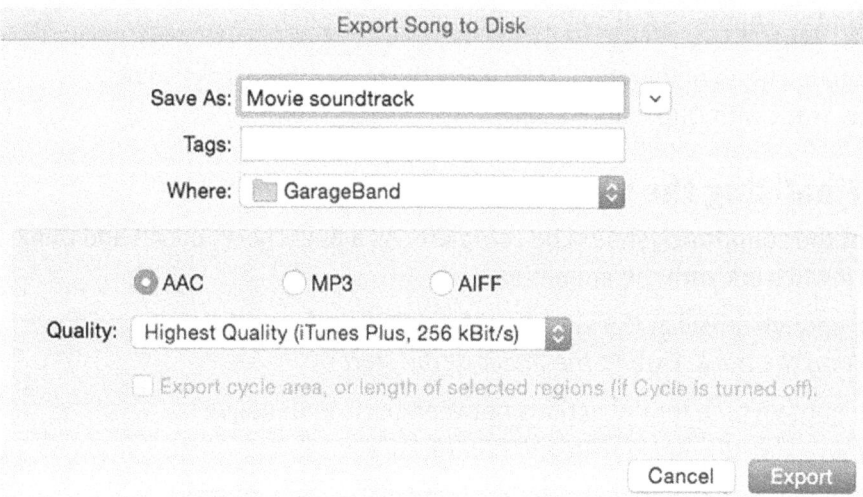

Because we are making a stop motion movie, it may make sense to create a new folder in the Movies folder and save all GarageBand, iStopMotion and iMovie files into it.

Recording with a microphone

GarageBand can record sounds, such as a voice, sound effects or music with a microphone. The audio clips are coloured blue and stored in 'Real Instrument' tracks.

It is very important to get the best quality sound recording you can (see *Sound versus noise* on page 56 and *Tips for great sound* on page 57).

Connect the microphone to your computer and turn it on.

Select GarageBand⇢Preferences and on the Audio/MIDI panel select the Output device where you want to hear the sound (Built-in output is the computer speakers), and the Input device for your microphone. Close the Preferences.

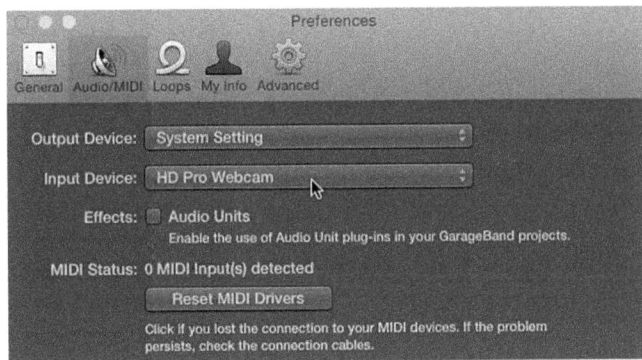

Microphone recordings are stored in an Audio track. If your project already has an Audio track, select the Track header *(it highlights in light grey)*, or to add an Audio track:

- Click the Add Track button ➕ above the top Track header ❸. Select Audio using a microphone and click 'Create', *or*
- CTRL-click a Track header and select 'New Audio Track'.

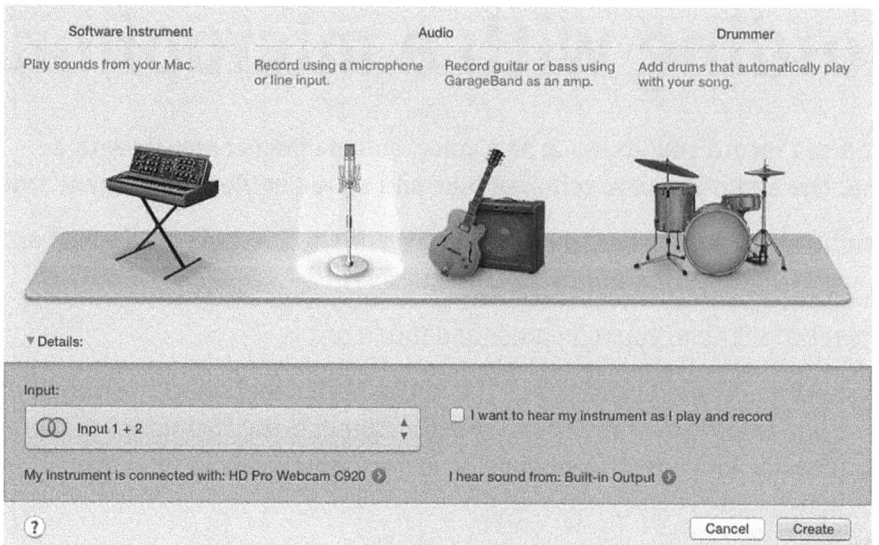

The Library automatically opens. Select the sound category from the left column, eg Voice, and the sound patch from the right column for the type of sound you want, eg Bright Vocal. This is a good option for recording dialogue. We can change this sound as part of editing. There are additional vocal sound patches in the Legacy category.

- Click the Library button 📇 (Y) to close the Library.

To check that the Audio track is connected to the microphone:

- Click the Smart Controls button 👣 (B)
- Click the Inspector button ⓘ in the Smart Controls panel

- Confirm your microphone is the one stated as the Input. If the microphone records in stereo, click the button to show double circles (one circle means mono recording)

If the waveform for the audio clip shows two lines, it is a stereo recording. However, if one line is flat with no waveform the microphone is only producing mono sound and will only play through one speaker. Change the Input to mono (one circle), and you'll only see one waveform line which will play equally through both left and right speakers

Stand when recording audio for better voice control

- Talk into your microphone and notice the recording level in the track header. Adjust the Record Level slider in the Inspector  so that as many green bars as possible are lit. When the sound gets very loud, the meter bars turn orange and then red. Red means that the volume is overloading the track, causing distortion or clipping.

You'll need to check the Record Level during every recording because every voice actor and expression may have a different volume.

Automatic Level Control lets the computer take over the task of adjusting the volume. It lowers the level to prevent distortion and raises the level if the sound is too quiet. However, if there is no sound for a short period, eg a silent gap between sentences, the noise may become too loud.

GarageBand includes a metronome which plays a steady beat to help you play music in time. It is not useful when recording dialogue and the beat will interfere with the microphone so turn off the Metronome . The Count-in 1234 is also not useful in recording dialogue, so turn this off as well *(neither button should be purple)*.

To record with a microphone:

- Select the Track header *(highlights in light grey)*
- Place the Playhead on the Ruler at the position you want to add the recording
- Press R or click the Record button – then speak the words, create the sound or play the music
- Press the spacebar or click the Stop button to stop recording.

To listen to your recording, move the Playhead back to the start of the Ruler and press the spacebar.

53

Assessing the quality of your soundtrack

You can get a good idea about the quality of the sound by looking at the shape of the waveform line, particularly the magnified view in the Editor ✂ (E). In general, you should see distinct sections of wavy or jagged lines when there should be sound and thin straight horizontal lines when there is silence.

The volume of a good clear recording can be adjusted without significantly increasing the noise. Use the volume slider in the Track header. Here is an example of a good recording.

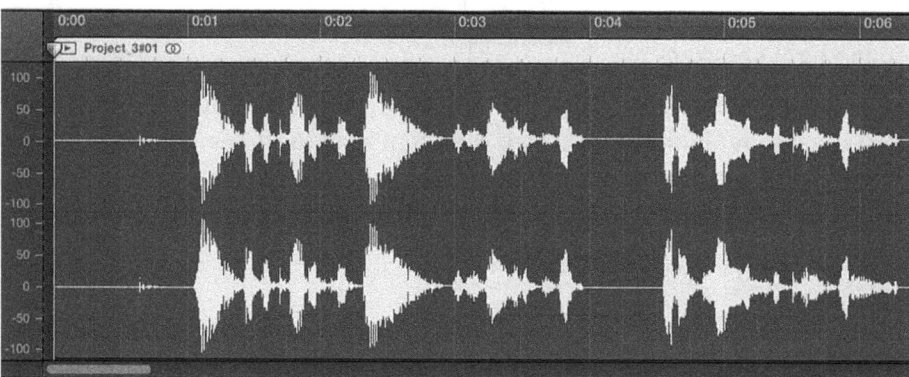

Too quiet

If the waveform lines are not very high, the sound may not be distinct from the background noise. However, increasing the volume of this sound will also make background noise louder.

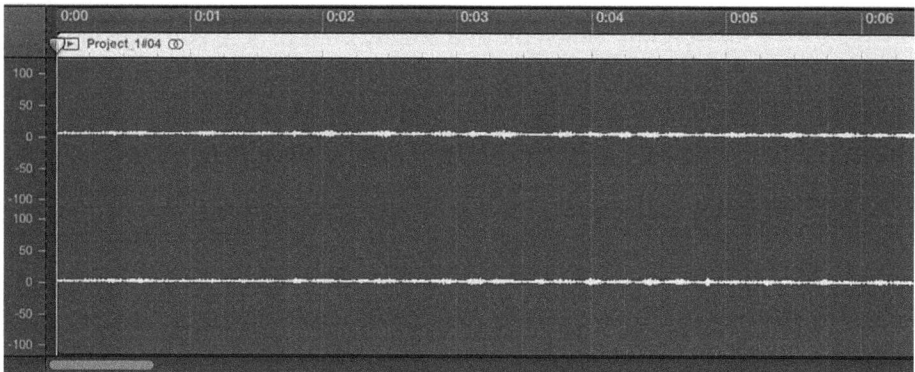

Solution: You'll need to record it again, but make sure you are recording from the correct microphone (see *Recording with a microphone* on page 51) then check the microphone selected as Input in the Inspector ⓘ in the Smart Controls 👣 (B). You may need to move the microphone closer to the sound, make the sound louder, adjust the Record Level or turn on Automatic Level Control.

Too loud

When the volume is very loud and the waveform reaches the top and bottom of sound path, it will be distorted and unpleasant to listen to. Reducing the volume of this sound will not remove the damage of the distortion.

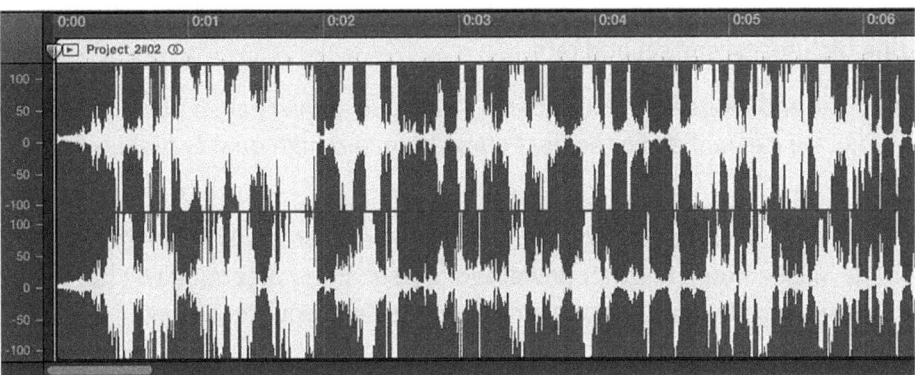

Solution: You'll need to record it again, but adjust the recording level or turn on Automatic Level Control, make the sound quieter or move the microphone away from the sound.

Editing Real Instrument tracks

To edit Real Instrument (blue) tracks see *Editing the soundtrack* on page 68.

Dot. Smallest stop motion
by Sumo Science and Aardman for Nokia

A 9mm girl called Dot struggles through a microscopic world. Recorded through a microscope attachment.
www.youtube.com/watch?v=CD7eagLl5c4

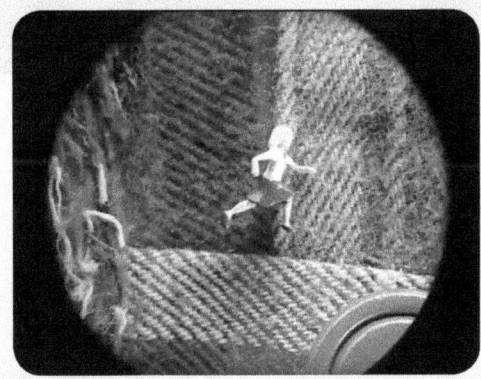
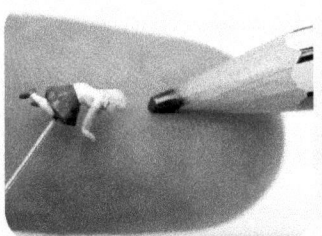
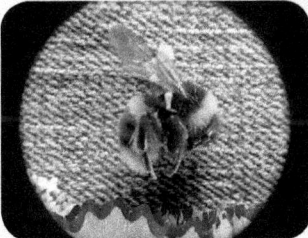

Dot. The making of.

Sound versus noise

Sound has a surprising effect on the quality of a movie. Clear and crisp sound can make bad picture look better than they are, whereas noisy and muffled sound will make amazing pictures 'seem' second rate.

Professional music and loops are recorded in a studio, so are very clear and vibrant. Without a studio, we can still make the best effort to record high quality dialogue to match.

When recording with a microphone, you want a clean, clear recording of the desired **'sound'** with the least amount of other unwanted **'noise'**. Every recording will have some noise. These steps help reduce the amount of noise in your recording:

- Take time to find the quietest location you can
- Listen for noises such as the drone of a computer or the tick of a wall clock and turn them off or take them out of the room. Think about potential noises – switch off your phone and take off that bracelet or rustling jacket
- Shut the doors and windows to block any noise from outside
- Wait for the plane to fly overhead or for the lawnmower next door to finish
- The remaining noise (drone of city traffic or wind in the trees) is the ambient noise you'll need to accept. However, you can **minimise the level of the ambient noise in relation to the sound level by moving the microphone as close as possible to the sound.** For example, if the sound is 1 metre away from the microphone, reducing the distance increases the sound level but does not increase the level of the noise, therefore the noise becomes less noticeable in the recording.

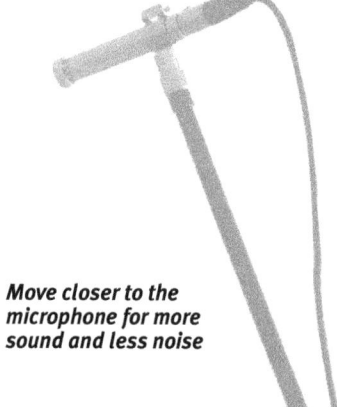

Move closer to the microphone for more sound and less noise

The microphone shown above is the *Oktava MK-012*.

Tips for great sound

- Use the best microphone and recording equipment you have access to (see *Microphones* on page 34 and *Equipment to record sound* on page 35)
- Point the microphone at the sound you want to record
- Use a microphone stand
- Use a rubber shockproof mount to help isolate the microphone from noises (see *How to make a microphone shock mount* on page 59). Avoid touching the cable as this may add 'unwanted noise' into the recording
- Listen to a test recording before recording the real thing. Assess the quality of your sound through high quality speakers such as your home stereo and not just through your computer speakers. Listen for the brightness and quality of the sound, as well as any underlying drone or hiss in the quiet parts
- Set the appropriate recording level. **Automatic** increases the sound level until there is a strong sound signal – often leading to loud background noises when there should be silence. On the other hand, the sound rarely distorts because the level is automatically reduced when it is too loud. **Manual** lets you set the level of sound usually giving a better, purer sound. But if you make a mistake, the recording may be too quiet to hear, or it may be too loud, distorted or unpleasant to listen to
- If your microphone has a battery, make sure you use a new battery
- If your microphone is close to a hard surface such as a wall, use soft furnishings such as cushions or carpet on the wall or floor to reduce sound reflections
- Using headphones may help you notice unwanted noise while recording. Be very critical – the bang of a door down the corridor when someone is talking cannot be fixed later. Record it again
- Use your fingers to count 3 seconds of silence before and after each recording so that you have extra background ambient silence when editing.

Clarity

The most common problem with recording dialogue is when voice actors speak too many words, too quickly.

In acted movies, we see the character's mouth movements so even slurred or muffled words can be understood (mostly). With stop motion, the audio needs to be much clearer because characters often have fixed mouth shapes. The clarity of the words need to come from the audio.

Instruct your voice actors to take care with their pronunciation. Make sure they open their mouth wide when talking. Don't take the personality out of the voice, but listen carefully for words that run together or where the diction is not clear, and record that part again. In particular, make sure the consonant sounds are crisp (I call this 'crunchy consonants'), and have a breath between sentences. It will be disappointing if your audience can't enjoy your movie because they have no idea what is said!

Larger than life

These final ideas will help bring your soundtrack to life:

- Have voice actors stand when recording as it is easier to breathe deeply and 'throw' your voice

- Coach voice actors in the tone and pace of the story for each line – should they be scared, happy, excited, shy or breathless? Most people will need to be strongly encouraged to find their most expressive voice. If it helps to remove distractions, suggest they close their eyes to imagine the situation their character is in

- Reading from a script can sound dull and uninteresting. Dramatic or 'acted' voices sound much better. Don't shout, but put expression into your voice

- Record the dialogue in short blocks. Try to memorise the words so you don't have to read them. If you need a printed reference of the script use large size text and pin it next to the microphone – but remember you want it 'acted' not 'read'

- It can be easier to start with just an outline of the key story points and prompt people to improvise their lines in their own words and with expression. Dramatic stories may require a different expression for every line. If the first take is not dramatic enough, immediately record another take, and another if necessary

- It can feel uncomfortable being overly expressive, but it will create a better movie. The dialogue in many TV sitcom programmes mostly consists of one liners (jokes). In one Disney show a laugh was scripted every 8 seconds. The characters don't just knock at the door and say 'I'm home'. It is more like **"I'M H O M E !!!"**. We're not suggesting every stop motion should be like a Disney show, but more expressive audio recordings will produce more engaging movies.

How to make a microphone 'shock' mount

Microphones pick up sounds through the air as well as physical noises transmitted through direct contact with stands, cables or people.

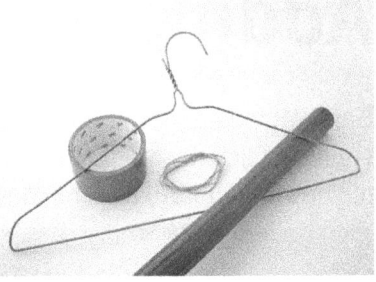

A shock mount helps to produce a cleaner audio recording because it suspends the microphone in the air, reducing contact with other objects.

You'll need a sturdy wire coathanger, rubber bands, tape and a long stick, such as a broom handle:

Step 1
Bend the **coathanger** to form a large 'U' shape

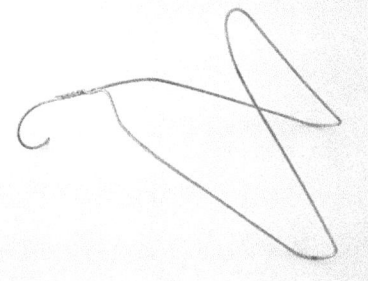

Step 2
Bend up a lip in the middle of the long side to give clearance for the end of the microphone

Step 3
Bend the coathanger hook around a **pole** and wrap with **tape** to fasten it

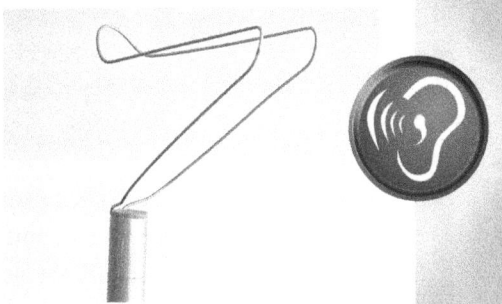

Step 4
Wrap **rubber bands** around the microphone and the wire. Make sure the microphone is freely suspended between the wires and not touching them.

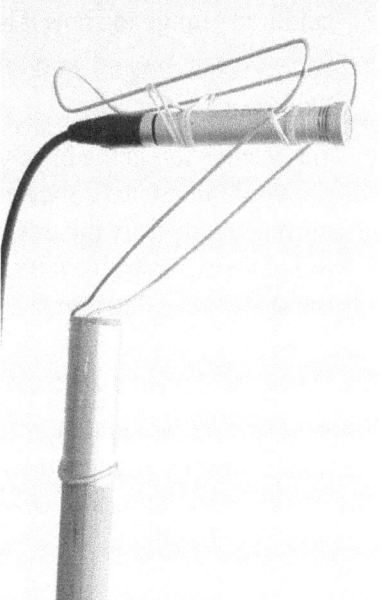

Adding other media

GarageBand soundtracks can include music and sounds from a wide range of other sources. Click the Media Browser button ![] (F) to show the songs from iTunes, and movies from iPhoto and the Movies folder.

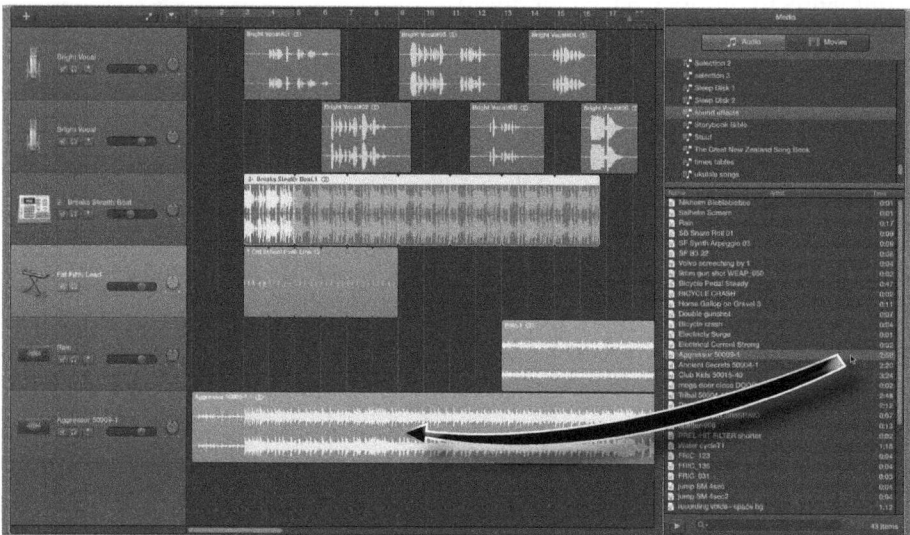

- The **Audio** tab in the browser shows music and sounds that are directly available in GarageBand. Select a **song or sound** and drag it into the required place in an Audio track (clips are coloured blue) or into the blank area at the bottom of the Workspace, and a new Audio track will automatically be created. The clip is coloured orange to show it is imported audio.

  You can also drag an audio file from the desktop directly into GarageBand's Workspace

- The **Movies** tab in the browser shows movies that are directly available to GarageBand. Select a **movie** and drag it into the Workspace (you can also drag a movie directly from the desktop) – a movie track will automatically be added at the top of the Workspace. You can only add one movie per GarageBand file. It begins at the start of the Ruler and cannot be offset to start at a different time.

Getting additional sound effects and music

When searching for audio files for the soundtrack, some sites give numbers indicating the quality of their sounds. Higher numbers generally indicate higher quality. The numbers are important when comparing one sound with another.

The **file size** may be an indicator of the potential quality of the sound, but there are other ways to assess the recording quality.

Here is more information about recording quality:

- Audio files can be in a range of formats including **WAV**, **AIFF**, and **MP3**. WAV and AIFF tend to be high quality and uncompressed, hence they are large files. MP3 files are compressed (data is removed from the file) and the quality of the file is determined by the amount of compression

- **Sample rate** - the number of times the sound was sampled per second. Look for sounds with a minimum of 44.1 khz, often regarding as CD quality. 48hkz is higher quality and regarded as DVD quality

- **Bits per sample** is the amount of sound information that is collected in a sample. 16 bits is better than 8 bits per sample

- **Bitrate** is the amount of sound information in the file. It can be calulated as the multiple of the sample rate and bits per sample (and whether the sound is mono or stereo). CD quality is 1,411,200 bits per second (1,411k).

    An MP3 with a bitrate of 320K is very high quality. An MP3 above 192K is likely to have enough quality. Free sound effects and music often have a much lower bitrate and should be avoided if you want the best quality.

Ultimately, the best way to assess the quality of the sound is to **listen carefully and decide whether you like the realism of the sound**. In particular, if the sound starts and ends with noise rather than silence it could be heavily compressed – perhaps avoid that one.

Over time, you may accumulate quite a few music and sound effect files.
Create suitably named playlists in iTunes to store them for easy access in future.

Sound effects

Sound effects (also known as Foley sounds) intensify the mood of the movie.
They make real things, such as a thunder clap, more dramatic. They can also add a new sensation, such as the spine chilling noise of steel on steel, when entering a dark room.

GarageBand has hundreds of sound effects available in the Loop Browser ☊ (O). Click the Sound Effects category button (see *Adding loops* on page 65) – you may need to drag the divider down to reveal all buttons.

GarageBand also has a Software Instrument for Sound Effects. Using one of the keyboard options (see page 67), every note plays a different sound effect. Sound effect categories include: Applause and Laughter, Comedy Noises, Nature Sounds and Radio Sounds.

With a good microphone you can record your own sounds – just be creative (see *Microphones* on page 34 and *Tips for great sound* on page 57). The people recording the sound effects for *Lord of the Rings* dragged a concrete block through a tunnel to get a deep echoey sound for one of their monsters. They also got 20,000 people at a sports match to cheer for a battle scene.

What do you think you could do to create sound effects for the following?

- A spaceship landing
- A wild chicken
- A giant walking
- A tree crying
- A whale call
- An earthquake.

An excellent reference for recording sound effects is *'The Sound Effects Bible'* by Ric Viers. It is written for big screen movie makers, but it contains many useful ideas to create your own sound effects with everyday items such as food.

Get extra sound effects by searching for *'royalty free sound effects'* or *'free sound effects'*. Your local library may also have royalty free sound effects on CD.

- Some sites give away **free** files as a sampler to entice you to buy packs of sounds. Other sites simply have free sounds to download. The quality of these sounds can range from excellent to very poor
- **Royalty free** means that once you have paid the appropriate fee, the music or sound effect is yours to use as you wish as often as you like with no further payment
- **Creative Commons** means an artist has chosen to make their work available to others as long as the terms are followed. Read the agreement before using the sound effect or music, eg you may need to give the artist credit.

Go to *www.stop-motion-handbook.com/pages/audio_resources.html* for links to excellent sites for sound effects and music (as well as discounts and coupon codes), such as:

- **Blastwave FX** has packs of themed sound effects including Heroes and Villains. If you're looking for one resource for action type sound effects this could be it. 1000 sound effects including weapons, impacts, crashes, explosions, vehicles, robots, super powers, ambiences and many more! Get your coupon code to save 20%.

If you're still undecided, check out their free download of sample sounds *(www.blastwavefx.com)*

- **Audioblocks** has sound effects, music and loops. This is a subscription-based site with an introductory offer of 7 days free then a low cost annual fee for unlimited downloads *(www.audioblocks.com)*. Get your coupon code to save.

- **Pro Sound Effects** specialise in sound effects. They offer individual sounds from $5, monthly plans and themed libraries of sounds *(www.prosoundeffects.com)*. Get your coupon code to save 20%.

- **Soundsnap** offers credit packs so you can choose the combination of sound effects you want *(www.soundsnap.com)*

- **Instant Sound FX** has a mega bundle of thousands of sounds in a single low cost purchase *(www.instantsoundfx.com)*

- **Sound Effects Library** provides searchable access to many different sound libraries *(www.sound-effects-library.com)*

- **Sound Bible** offers free sound effects and royalty free sound effects licensed under Creative Commons *(www.soundbible.com)*

- **Freesound** is a collaborative database of free sounds licensed under Creative Commons *(www.freesound.org)*

- **Audio Micro** has free and royalty free sound effects *(www.audiomicro.com)*

- **FreeSFX** offers a free download of sound effects. Many sounds are provided by leading sound sites, but at a lower quality *(www.freesfx.co.uk)*

- **Find Sounds** searches the internet for free sounds of various quality *(www.findsounds.com)*

- **Flash Kit** offers shareware and freeware sounds *(www.flashkit.com/soundfx)*.

Music

Music creates identity for your stop motion. It can change of the tone of the story, so take care to choose the right type of music.

These are some of the different types of music which are used for different purposes in a stop motion:

- **Theme tune** – a full length tune which features different parts such as an introduction, verse, chorus, bridge and an ending. Theme tunes add a unique feel to the stop motion so it is important to choose an appropriate tune. The volume may need to be reduced when there is dialogue

- **Stinger** -- a very short tune useful at the start of a scene, between scenes, or to draw attention

- **Underscore** – a quiet tune which is designed to play under dialogue
- **Loop** – a short tune designed to repeat without creating an obvious join
- **Atmosphere (ambience** or **soundscape)** – long recording of the sounds heard in a particular location such as at park, cafe, train station or in space.

The best music for stop motion will probably be instrumental. Don't use popular music from the radio or YouTube because the words make it hard to fit in with your dialogue. Also, you'll need to permission to use it.

GarageBand has hundreds of music clips available in the Loop Browser Ω (O). Click the Jingles category button (see *Adding loops* on page 65).

Get extra music by searching for *'royalty free music'* or *'free music for video'*. Your local library may have royalty free music on CD.

Here are some excellent sites for free and royalty free music:

- **Freeplay Music** has 15,000 songs that can be used in the classroom and for personal use on YouTube *(www.freeplaymusic.com)*
- **Free Stock Music** sign up for a free account to download free music. These are high quality tunes provided as an introduction to Audioblocks.com so there are a few pop up windows to navigate *(www.freestockmusic.com)*
- **Audioblocks** has music, loops and sound effects. It is a subscription-based site with introductory offer of 7 days free then a low cost annual fee for unlimited downloads *(www.audioblocks.com)*
- **Purple Planet** has royalty free and free music *(www.purple-planet.com)*
- **Free Music Archive** is a forum for artists to upload free music for others to use *(www.freemusicarchive.org)*
- **MusOpen** is a non-profit site focussed on increasing access to music with free resources. It has classical and royalty free music licensed under Creative Commons *(www.musopen.org)*
- **Audiojungle** has royalty free music. Sign up for the free file of the month *(www.audiojungle.net)*
- **Dig CC Mixter** has music licensed under Creative Commons *(http://dig.ccMixter.org)*.

There are many other sites which have music files including *www.music-for-video.com*, *www.neumannfilms.net*, *www.ibaudio.com* and *www.dawnmusic.com*.

Adding loops

Loops are very short pre-recorded beats, rhythms or tunes. Loops can be repeated (looped) and combined with other loops to make up a song. GarageBand comes with thousands of loops and you can buy more to extend the range. Search for *Apple Jam Packs* (Voices, Rhythm Section, World Music, Remix Tools, Symphony Orchestra) or for *'GarageBand loops'*.

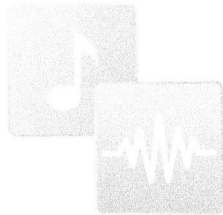

Loops with a **green icon** are made with synthetic Software Instruments. If they are added to a Software Instrument track, the sound can be changed to play with a different instrument, eg from a piano to a choir, french horn or harp. If they are added to an Audio track they are converted into a microphone recording.

Loops with a **blue icon** have been recorded by real instruments with a microphone. They can only be added to an Audio track.

To add loops:

- Click the Loop Browser button  (O)
- Select the category buttons for the type of instrument (guitar, keyboard, percussion...), genre (rock, electronic...) and mood (distorted, melodic...).
  You may have to drag the divider down to reveal all the buttons. The loops that match your description are listed
- Click a loop to hear it. Click it again to turn it off

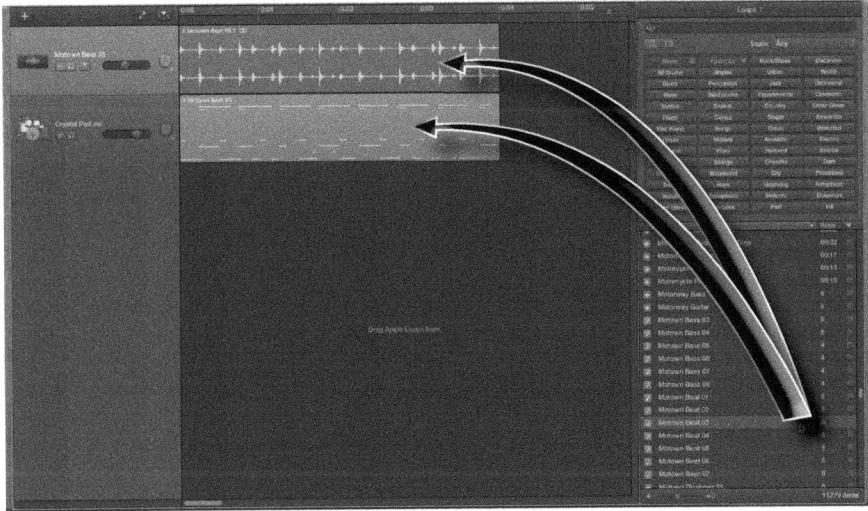

- Drag a loop into the required place in a track (of the right kind – blue or green) or into the blank area at the bottom of the Workspace to create a new track.

65

Editing loops

- To **move a loop,** click the centre of the loop and drag it to a new position – either along the same track or into a new track of the same type of instrument (software or real)

- To make a **loop longer,** hold your mouse over the top right corner of the loop until the cursor becomes a curved arrow, then drag it to the longer length you want and the loop will automatically repeat to fit the length

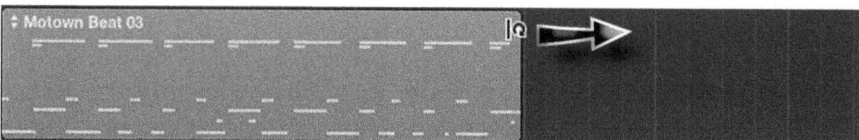

- To make a **loop shorter,** hold your mouse over the bottom right corner of the loop until the cursor becomes a double arrow slider then drag it to the shorter length you want

- Many loops have alternative versions. Click the name of a loop in a track to see a list of other loops with a similar sound. Using these alternative loops is a good way of creating musical variety. Instead of adding a loop and extending it to repeat, add several copies of one loop and change some to alternative loops

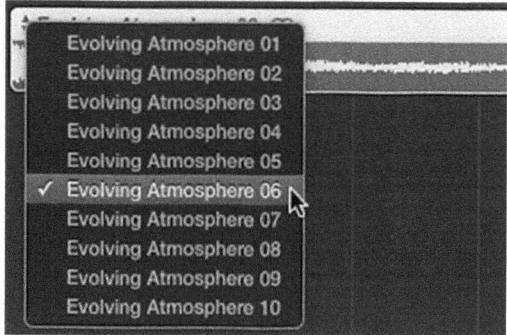

- Loops are designed to play together to create a richer sound. If the Loop Browser states the beats as 4, 8 or 16, simply align the start of the loops and they will play in time

- The actual notes in Software Instrument loops *(coloured green)* can be edited (see *Editing software instruments* on page 70).

Software Instruments

A Software Instrument track (coloured green) is like a page of music notes. It contains information about which note is played and for how long. The actual instrument can be changed.

To create sounds and music with software instruments:

- Click the New Track button ➕ and add a keyboard or guitar track in the Workspace (*clips will be coloured green*)
- From the Library 🗄 (Y) select the appropriate settings for the instrument category from the left column and the patch from the right column for the type of sound you want
- Plug in a musical keyboard or instrument with a USB connection

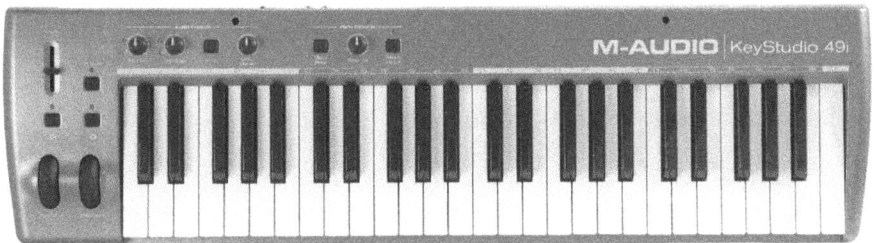

or use one of GarageBand's keyboards – Window⋯▸Keyboard, or (CMD-K for musical typing)

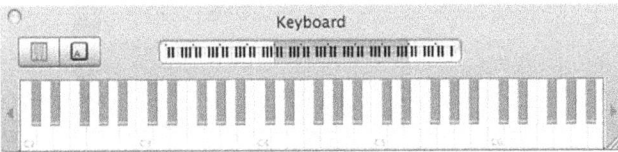

- Turn on the Metronome 🎼 and Count-in 1234 if they will be useful when recording music *(both buttons should be purple)*
- Position the Playhead on the Ruler where you want to start recording
- Click the Record button or press R – then play the music on the instrument
- Press the spacebar or click the Stop button to stop recording.

Editing Software Instrument tracks

To edit Software Instrument (green) tracks see *Editing the soundtrack* on page 68.

Editing the soundtrack

When you have recorded the lines of dialogue or sound effects, follow this process to edit them for use in a soundtrack:

- Trim audio clips
- Move clips along the tracks so they play at the right time with other clips and the soundtrack flows
- Make precise editing changes using the Editor  (E)
- Apply effects to enhance the sound.

Increase the zoom magnification to assist accuracy when editing.

Trimming

The first step to tidy up a soundtrack is to delete parts of audio clips with mistakes or accidental noises:

- Click the Solo button in the track you want to edit
- Click an audio clip to select it
- Place the Playhead where you want to trim the clip. This is just a rough first cut so don't trim too close to the start or end of the actual sound
- Select Edit⇢Split Regions at Playhead (CMD-T).

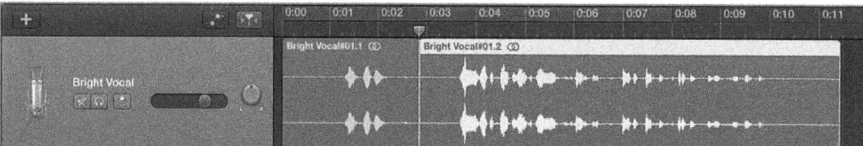

Alternatively, if you want to trim the end of the clip, click and drag the end to shorten the clip.

Both methods only hide the trimmed parts. To recover trimmed parts click and drag the end to lengthen the clip.

Moving

From the start of the Ruler, move clips along the tracks so they play at the right time with other clips and the soundtrack flows. If you have made specific volume changes in the automation track, make sure these move with the audio clip – select Mix⇢Move Track Automation with Regions.

Click the centre of a clip and drag it to a new position:

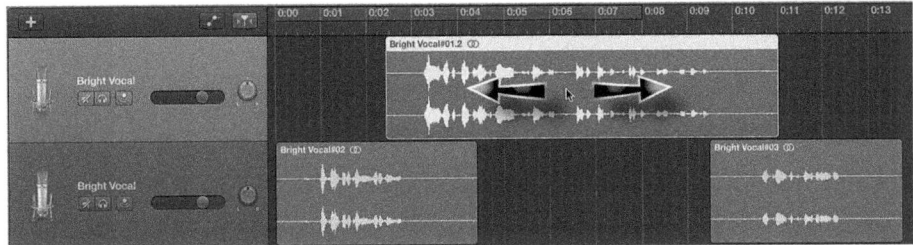

- To increase the gap between sounds, eg lines of dialogue, place the Playhead in a silent gap and press CMD-T to split the audio clip into two. Drag the right half of the clip towards the right to create a gap
- To decrease the gap between sounds or have several sounds play at the same time, create a new Audio track, drag the second clip into the new track and move it to play at the right time.

Precise editing in the Editor window

Double-click an audio clip or click the Editor button  (E) to show a magnified view. This makes it easier to set precise points for trimming, moving/aligning clips and changing the volume. Use the Editor's horizontal zoom to further increase the magnification.

In this example, note the small 'blip' of sound at the start of the clip (circled). This is likely to be noise – maybe knocking the microphone or a tap on the keyboard:

- Click the Automation button  to reveal the volume line for each track
- In the Editor, place the Playhead just after this 'blip'
- Click an edit point on the track volume line
- Drag the edit point down to reduce the volume at this point.

Check the start and end of every clip and adjust the automation volume line to remove all unwanted noises. This will clean up the soundtrack and dramatically improve its quality. **The more unwanted sounds and noise you can remove from audio clips, the clearer the soundtrack will be.**

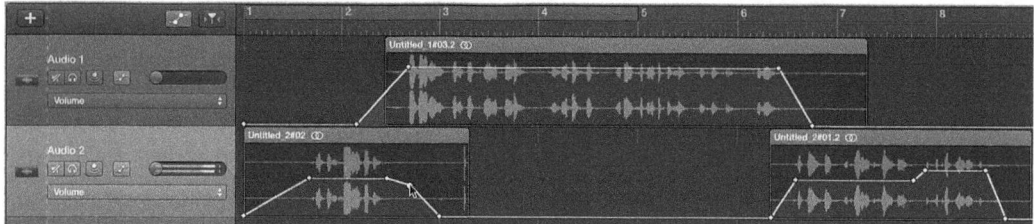

Editing software instruments

Music recorded using Software Instruments can be edited, note by note.

Double-click a clip or click the Editor button ✂ (E) to see your music either like a piano roll or as notes on a music score. Remember to use the horizontal zoom to assist accuracy when editing:

- To move a note to a different pitch or to change the timing, click the bar or note and drag it to the correct position

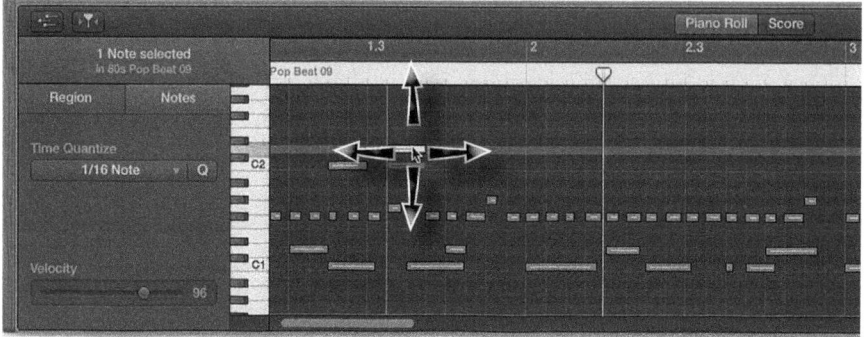

- To change the length of the note, click the right end of the bar or note and drag it (longer or shorter) to the required length
- To add a new note, hold CMD as you click and drag the pencil cursor to create the new note.

The type of software instrument selected for a track can be changed in the Library (Y) after it has been recorded.

Editing the soundtrack later

If, while recording the pictures for your stop motion, you decide the soundtrack needs to be changed:

- Open the original GarageBand file (**the master**)
- Make the changes. If you change the timing of the soundtrack up to the point where you have recorded pictures, you may need to record those pictures again or edit the picture sequence in iStopMotion. If you don't change the timing of the soundtrack, it will continue to line up perfectly with your pictures
- Save the GarageBand file – File⟶Save. **This is your new master**
- Select Share⟶Export Song to Disk to save the replacement soundtrack as an audio file (see *Saving the soundtrack* on page 50)
- In iStopMotion, click the button in the Soundtrack panel on the View pane to replace the soundtrack with the new one (see *Importing soundtrack* on page 118).

For an advanced stop motion process (used in big screen movies) create a basic dialogue only soundtrack in GarageBand to assist recording the pictures in iStopMotion. After all the stop motion pictures are recorded, import the movie into GarageBand so you can watch the movie as you add music and sound effects:

- In iStopMotion, turn the soundtrack off – move the slider left on the Soundtrack panel
- Save your movie File⟶Export (select the Movies folder on your computer)
- Open the original GarageBand file (the master)
- In GarageBand select the Media Browser button (F)
- In the Movies panel, select your movie and drag it into the Workspace, or drag the movie from the desktop
- Add other audio such as sound effects and music, or apply Plug-in effects while you watch your movie
- Save the GarageBand file – File⟶Save. **This your new master**
- Save your movie. Select Share⟶Export Movie to Disk.

Props and set up

This chapter covers many aspects that support making good stop motion. You will learn about:

- Modelling with Plasticine
- Building with LEGO®
- Setting up a stop motion stage
- Tips for great pictures
- Camera, tripod and mount
- Lighting
- How to make a portable stage.

Modelling with Plasticine

Plasticine modelling clay can be purchased at art supply shops in a range of colours. Colours can be mixed together to create new colours.

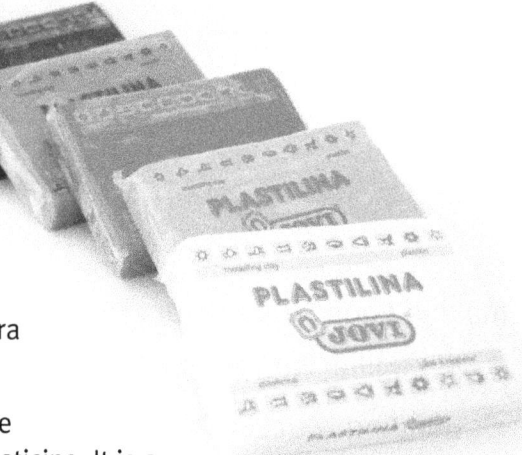

Take care not to contaminate the various colours of Plasticine. Wash your hands regularly, particularly when working with light coloured Plasticine. Clean hands will also help keep your computer and camera free of Plasticine marks.

Put a layer of plastic over the table. Don't use newspaper because the ink will stain the Plasticine. It is a good idea to put a covering on the floor.

Plasticine modelling tools

Many kitchen utensils are useful for creating Plasticine characters. You'll probably want to get your own set so you don't get Plasticine in your food. Check in the kitchen for spares or look in second-hand shops before you buy specialist tools from an art supply shop. You will need:

- A rolling pin. A 400mm offcut of 50mm PVC plumbing pipe works well
- A cutting surface such as a chopping board
- Blunt wooden and plastic tools for general moulding
- Sharper tools for adding fine details
- Cling film or plastic bags for wrapping unused Plasticine to keep it clean
- An old overshirt to keep your clothes clean
- A cloth for cleaning up when you are finished.

Making an armature Plasticine character

You will need some bendable wire (20 gram or 0.9mm thickness), pliers, bonding compound, rubber gloves for safety and, of course, some Plasticine.

Step 1
Create a simple **wire** skeleton for your character. The joints can be floppy at this stage.

Step 2
Put on **rubber gloves** and use a **bonding compound** to solidify the joints and to add mass to the skeleton. Leave wire exposed in the places that you want your character to bend, eg elbows and knees.

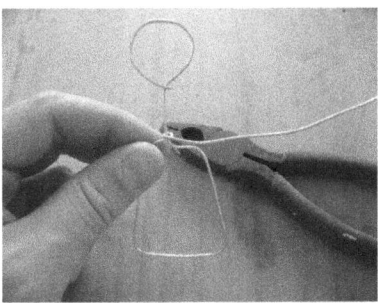

It can be a good idea to cover the wire with **fabric tape** with a furry surface, such as a bandage strip, to give a better surface for the Plasticine to stick to.

Step 3
Cover the skeleton with **Plasticine**.

Make sure the feet are solid and the body is balanced so the character can easily stand.

Step 4
Smooth and shape the character. Add other colours and mould fine details.

Step 5
Add details such as **beads** for eyes.

Plasticine – let your imagination run wild

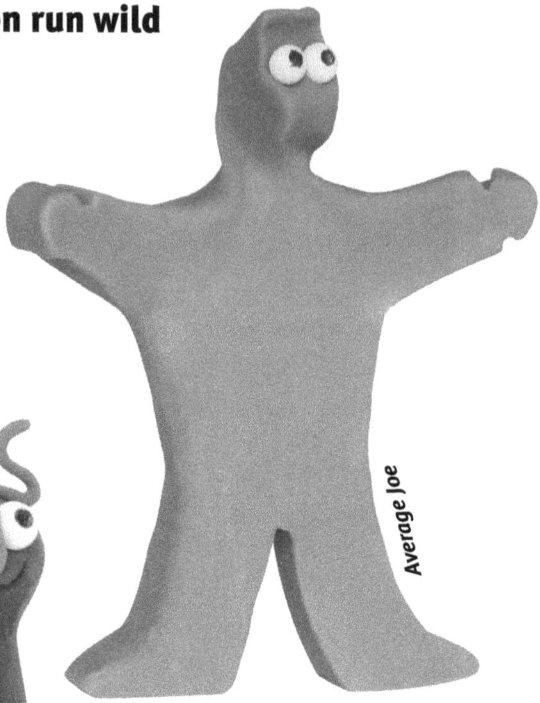

Average Joe

Tips:

- If you want a character to move, use an armature to strengthen the arms and legs
- Where possible, use beads for eyes because they won't lose their shape. Eyes are the 'windows to the soul' and give characters life
- Characters need solid feet and sturdy legs. Aim for a low centre of gravity so the character can easily stand and remain balanced when moving
- Use a lightweight object, such as polystyrene, to give mass to the body without weight
- Make fine detail items such as badges, ties, belts, etc out of a more solid modelling material such as Fimo.

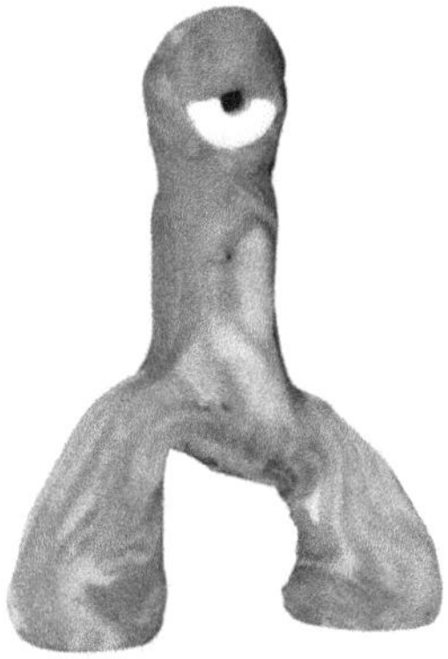

2D Plasticine characters

This method uses a 'cookie cutter' to quickly produce identical Plasticine characters. This is useful where you need lots of similar looking characters. It is also useful where you need to bend or distort the character, eg roll it into a ball, then use the same character again in the next scene.

With identical Plasticine characters you can have more than one group working on different scenes in the same movie.

Step 1
Roll Plasticine about 1.5cm thick.

Step 2
Make a 'cookie cutter' for your character. Use long nose pliers to bend a strip of thin metal into the shape of your character. You could also use a 'gingerbread man' cookie cutter from the kitchen.

Step 3
Press the shape into the Plasticine to cut out the character. Cut out as many characters as you need.

Step 4
Smooth the edges by hand, and make sure the character has solid square feet so it can stand.

Step 5
Add details such as beads for eyes.

Check out the adventures of Average Joe, a contender for the job as the world's next superhero, in his own animated comic strip: *www.acumen.net.nz/pages/NMSAverageJoe.html*

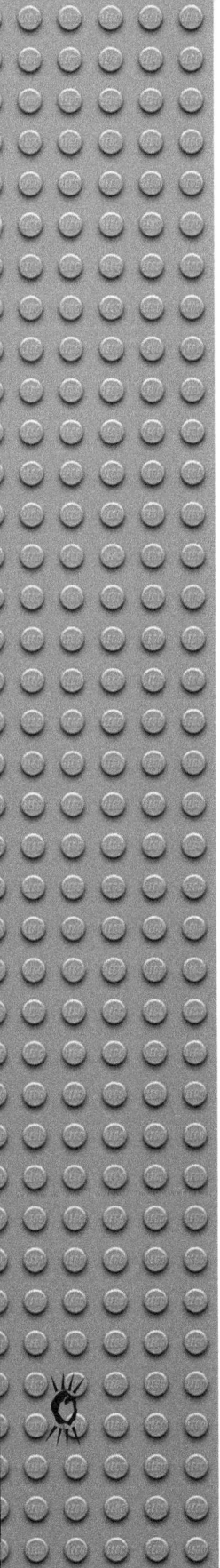

Building with LEGO

When working with LEGO®, you will need lots of LEGO® blocks, LEGO® minifigures and large LEGO® base boards.

- Store LEGO® minifigures in a separate container so printed details such as faces don't get scratched
- Take care to use LEGO® blocks which are in good condition and do not show signs of wear or damage
- Secure LEGO® base boards to the table or 'stage' with strong tape to prevent accidental movement. Duct tape (also called cloth or gaffer tape) works well because it has good stick and peels off cleanly
- If the ground under a minifigure is out of view, use whatever blocks are required to raise the minifigure to a good position in front of the camera
- Use a very small amount of Blu-Tack to position LEGO® minifigures at exaggerated angles
- Moving a LEGO® minifigure, or its limbs, is a very delicate movement. Brace yourself with your elbows firmly on the table so you can safely lean over your set to move the character without moving other parts of the set
- Join several LEGO® base boards together to create a stage with many viewpoints, such as a long perspective looking down a road or an aerial panorama. A long road can also be moved past the camera
- Build LEGO® buildings with a removable front wall which can easily be removed for inside scenes
- If you don't want to use LEGO® base boards, lay a sheet of metal, such as a whiteboard under a printed or painted background. Insert small magnets in the feet of the minifigures to assist movements, particularly when they are not standing vertical.

Setting up a stop motion stage

You can set up a stage for stop motion on a table or floor. It can be as big as a room but if you are working with small props such as LEGO® use a table (see *How to make a portable stage* on page 104). You just need enough space to move around your stage without accidentally bumping your camera. Use duct tape to secure the backgrounds to the stage so they don't move.

Here are some examples of stage set ups:

Standard stage with painted background

Use any medium you like to paint or create a background design or picture on a large sheet of card (eg A2-size). Add details at an appropriate scale for your characters (see *Determining the scale* on page 83):

- Position characters at the front of the stage so the camera focus will separate them from the background (see *Make your stop motion look like a 'film'* on page 90)
- For close-ups, raise characters on blocks to get a better camera angle or image composition
- Place props along the back of the stage to hide the horizon line
- Change the background during your movie to create scene changes.

Wide stage

If you have access to very large sheets of cardboard you can create wide backgrounds which cover the back of the stage and curve around the sides in a 'U' shape. This allows the camera to be moved to many vantage points without running out of background. This is particularly useful in action sequences where you need to move the camera a lot (see *How to dramatise an action sequence* on page 143).

Duct tape, also called cloth tape

Invisible horizon stage

Use a very large sheet of card (eg A1-size) to make a one-piece background, curved for the back and base of your stage.

This gives a great feeling of reality in your stop motion because there are no visible joins between sheets so it creates a natural horizon (see *Determining the scale* on page 83).

Green screen stage

Green screen is the technique of recording pictures in front of a coloured background and having that colour replaced with a photo (see *Adding a background* on page 156).

The two main requirements for a successful green screen are:

- A pure colour background. Any solid colour can be used although the colours chroma blue or chroma green work the best.

  Chroma blue and green cardboard is available from art supply shops. These colours are also available as paint from paint suppliers

- Bright and even lighting across the background (see *Lighting* on page 100).

Determining the scale between character and background

- Temporarily place the background card onto the stage
- Place the character on the stage and position your camera
- Look through the camera and draw pencil markings on the background indicating:

   A) **Maximum visible height:** – Zoom out for wide camera angle. Keep important details below this line or they won't be seen

   B) **Projected character head height**: – A useful reference for the scale height of buildings, trees

   C) **Horizon area**: – You don't want to create an actual horizon line, but you do need to know the point in the distance at which to start putting vertical details such as buildings.

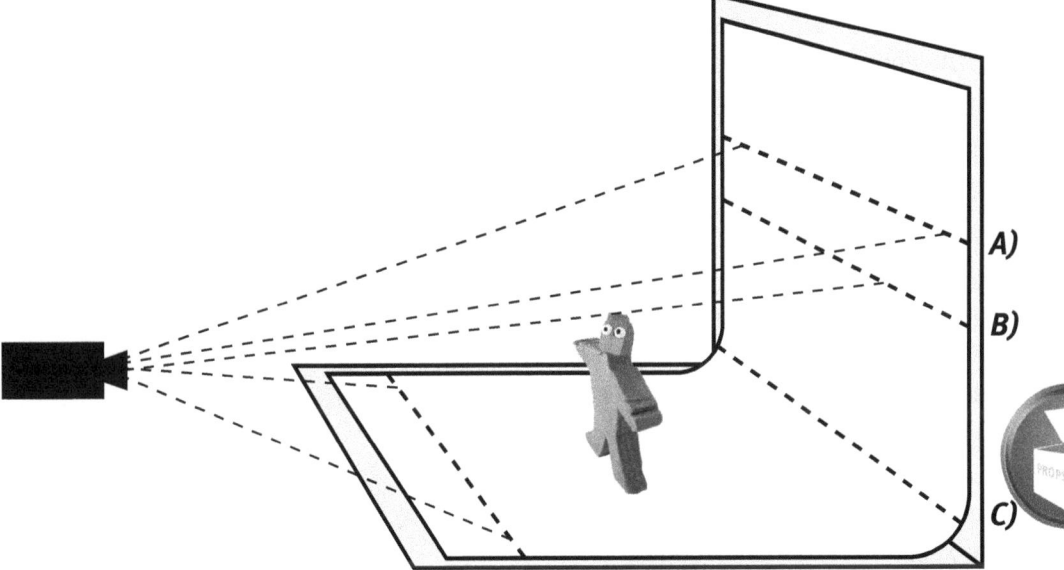

Flat stage

A stop motion stage can also be two dimensional – usually flat on a table. A vertical stage can be used where the artwork is on a wall, such as a whiteboard.

Mount the camera directly above or in front of the background so camera view is not distorted and the edge of the background is not in visible.

In the example shown a remote camera (iPad) is used. See also *How to fly a rocket* on page 137 and *Flat 2D animation* on page 148.

Creating a three dimensional world

A picture of a character standing directly in front of a background can look two dimensional. However, with a few props you can create a realistic three dimensional set for your character to move in and around.

Cut cardboard shapes for trees, building frontages and other props which will create depth and scale.

The city

In a city you are surrounded with alternative views every way you look. Buildings look different when you change perspective.

A stage for a stop motion in the city also needs a range of angles and views:

- Paint a simple sky background – graduating from bright blue (for day) to dark blue (for night). The graduation also gives a nice perspective towards the horizon and by rotating the background gives a day scene and a night scene
- Create city blocks with folded cardboard cutouts of building profiles. Use hidden supports and blocks behind the cutouts to keep them standing straight
- Paint a simple road system
- Keep the camera angle low so the buildings tower above the characters
- Remove a city block as needed for alternative camera angles.

The jungle

When walking through bush or jungle, stepping through one layer of trees reveals another layer behind in an ever changing view.

A stage for a stop motion in the jungle also needs layers of backgrounds:

- Paint a jungle background and a skyline. The colours should be muted and the detail soft or blurry
- Cut out several layers of jungle middle ground which your characters can walk between and hide behind. These should be colourful and include detailed plants.

Tips for great pictures

Picture composition

The arrangement of the characters and props on your stage is called composition. Every time you set up, or move your camera, check:

- Is the camera view interesting?
- Can the main character or object be easily seen?
- Are other characters or objects clearly placed and well spaced? In particular, check that objects aren't blocking each other from view.
- Are any elements arranged in a confusing way? eg does a tree appear to be coming out of someone's head?

Which of these pictures have good composition?

Because a movie is more than one picture, anticipate character movements so that you don't need to move the camera too often (see *Rule 1* on page 122). For example, if a giraffe is to walk onto the stage make sure that its head will fit into the camera view.

Look out for dirt and hairs on your sets and characters. Spots of dirt may be small, but when magnified through the camera can look huge. Clean your sets and characters with a cloth and small soft brush, and when working with Plasticine make sure you have clean hands.

The 'rule of thirds'

Which of these pictures looks the best?

The middle picture has good vertical balance. The character's head is not squashed into the top of the screen, and it is not drowning off the bottom of the screen.

Position the camera so that the character's eyes are one third down the screen for good composition.

To assist with picture composition, turn on iStopMotion's Grid (see *View options* on page 127) and set the columns and rows to 3.

The 'rule of thirds' applies in many situations and helps to give well balanced composition. In these next pictures, the eyes are about one third of the way down the screen. Regardless of the magnification, the picture will look balanced if they character's eyes are about one third down the screen.

Action safe

Some cameras and the iStopMotion software (shown below) display guidelines to assist picture composition. In iStopMotion the Action Safe guideline (see *View options* on page 127) displays a thin rectangle on the screen as a guide to help keep characters and important details away from the edge of the screen.

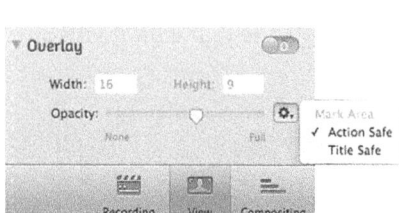 

Camera angle

Generally, have the camera lens level with the character's face.

- To make your characters look very tall, position the camera slightly lower so that it is looking up at the characters. You may need to raise characters on blocks to get the right angle
- To make your characters look short, position the camera slightly higher so that it is looking down at them.

When recording characters side on, slightly turn their heads towards the camera to reveal at least one eye for a more engaging picture.

Camera focus

Have you ever seen a picture where some parts are sharp and in focus and other parts are blurry? This is called 'depth of field'.

Cameras use a feature called 'focus' to select which part of the picture is sharp. There are two focus options:

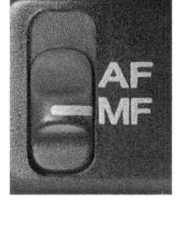

- **Automatic (AF)** – the camera decides what is in focus, and usually tries to make everything in focus
- **Manual (MF)** – YOU decide what is in focus.

Automatic focus usually does a good job, but sometimes the results are unpredictable. In the following two pictures, the focus has changed from the character (in the foreground) to the whale's tail (in the background). If this focus change happens randomly you will end up with a very messy movie.

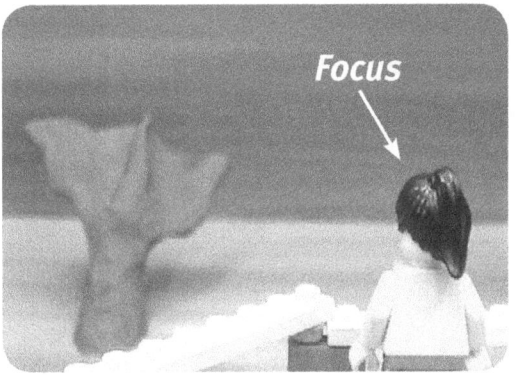
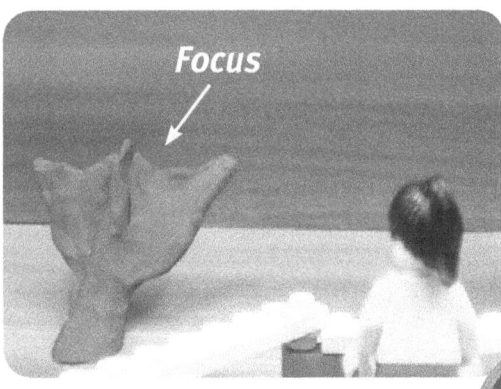

Manual focus is a much better way to make stop motion. Switch the camera to manual focus and then adjust focus so the important character or object has sharp detail.

The iPhone 4 and later, and 3rd gen iPad and later, have a manual focus feature which is controlled directly from iStopMotion.

Some remote cameras (eg iPad 2 and iPod Touch) use another focus method called fixed focus (see page 95).

How to focus

In general, set focus on the character's eyes. View the picture on the computer screen rather than trying to peer into the camera viewfinder.

If you can't clearly see whether a small detail is in focus, place another item with large crisp detail, such as a book cover, next to it. This will give you confidence that you have good focus.

Make your stop motion look like a 'film'

Big screen movies use techniques which make the background blurry, yet the characters are sharp and crisp.

To get the best result from the focus:
- Place the talking character much closer to the camera than to the background
- Increase the distance between the talking character and other characters/props
- Don't place important characters or props against the background.

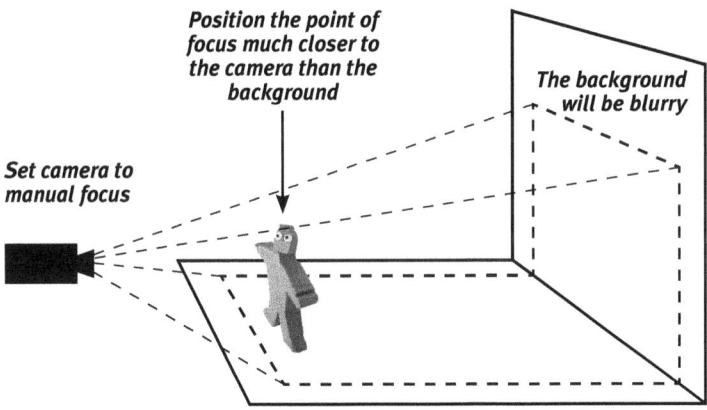

Backgrounds can be colour laserprints of photo scenes. Use the largest page size you have access to, to allow a range of camera angles.

Backgrounds don't need a lot of detail, particularly if they are to appear blurry. Having several backgrounds with patchy neutral tones in different colours is very useful. Gradients from a light colour to a dark colour are also useful. Paint your own backgrounds on large sheets of card (A2 is ideal).

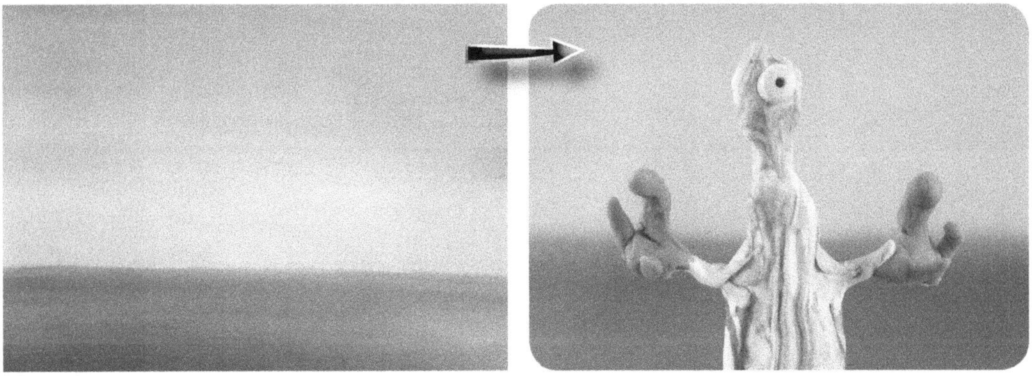

Behind the scenes

These pictures show that the camera view is often unrelated to the actual stage set. Stages don't need to be big and they don't need to be complete or tidy either. The only important thing is what the camera sees. Use props, supports, tape and other creative methods to position your character at the right height for the camera and in front of the background.

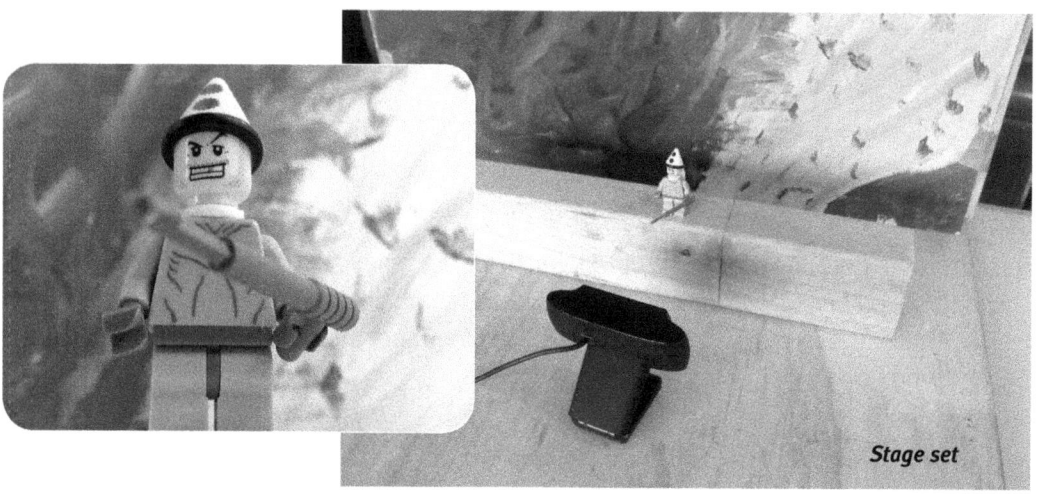

Stage set

Stage set

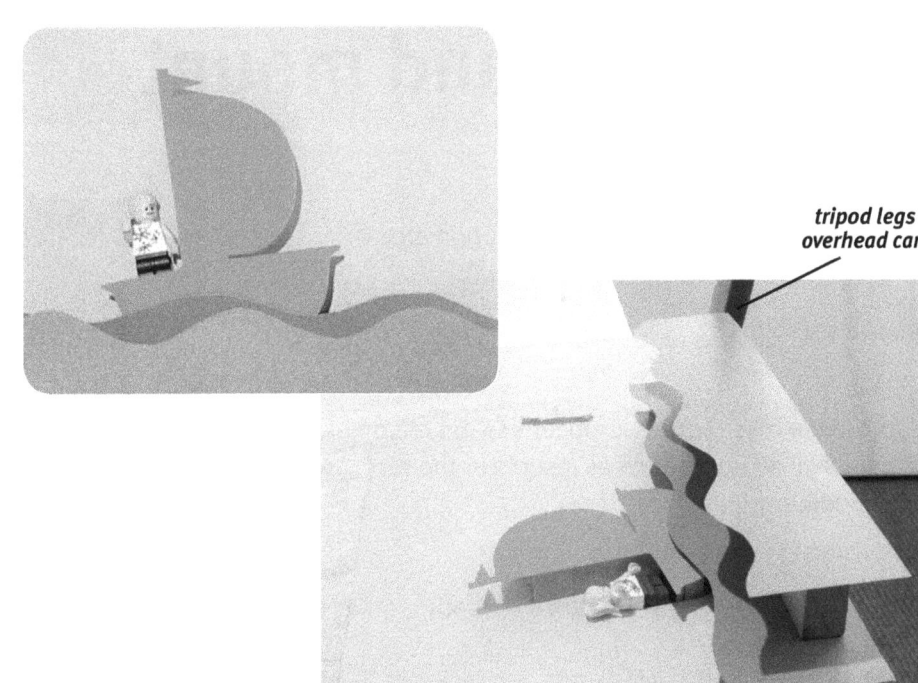

tripod legs for overhead camera

Stage set

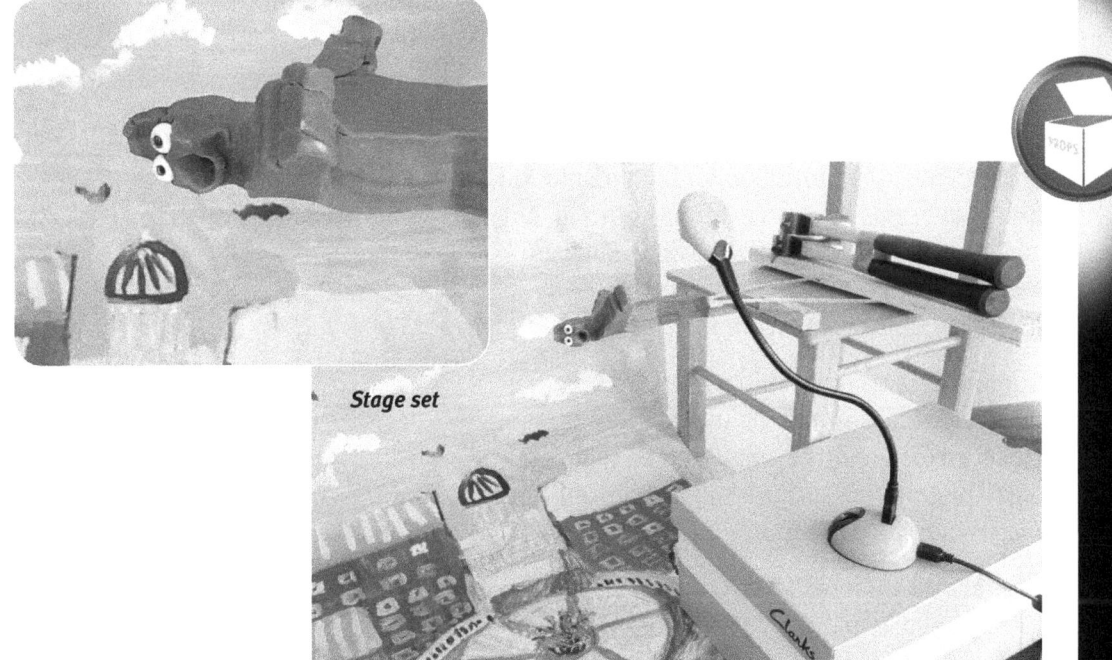

Stage set

Camera, tripod and mount

Choosing a camera for stop motion

The most important camera features for stop motion are:

- Manual focus (MF) – vital for the close-up work
- White balance setting
- Exposure setting
- Macro feature, or a macro or close-up lens to get crisp clear pictures of small items such as insects or the face of a LEGO® minifigure
- Quality of lens and camera optics.

If your camera has an image stabiliser, turn this feature off as it can affect the alignment of the pictures.

The number of mega-pixels is not important because HD TV is only 2 mega-pixels (standard TV is less than 1 mega-pixel). Many cameras (even up to 10 years old) fit this requirement so you don't need to spend a lot of money on the latest model.

Cameras

USB webcams are popular and cheap. The model shown is the *Logitech HD Pro c920* which has a glass lens for high quality pictures and can record up to 1080p for high resolution. Some webcams have no external controls, but can be adjusted with software apps such as *Webcam Settings (App Store)*, or *iGlasses (www.ecamm.com/mac/iglasses)*.

Some webcams may not have features such as manual focus, so won't be useful for producing close-up pictures. They may also be limited to a small picture size such as 640 x 480 pixels (see *Picture size* on page 108).

Digital still cameras (DSLR) are an excellent choice for high quality movies because of the quality and range of lenses available with these cameras. To see which cameras work with iStopMotion go to *https://boinx.com/connect/istopmotion/supportedcameras*.

Most **MiniDV video cameras** with a Firewire connection are compatible with iStopMotion. A high quality lens, such as 3CCD, can produce high quality pictures. Recent Macs no longer have a Firewire port.

The **iSight** camera on your computer has limited use for stop motion (see *Time lapse* example on page 150) as it lacks manual focus and zoom and is hard to get close to the action on your stage.

Stop motion can also be made from a series of digital picture files (see *Stop motion with a digital still camera* on page 159). Pictures can be taken on any digital device – camera, phone, MP3 player – as long as they can be uploaded to a computer. The camera does not have to be compatible with iStopMotion.

Remote camera

The rear camera in **iOS devices (iPad, iPhone or iPod Touch)** can be used as a wireless remote camera. The devices need to be:

- Connected to the same network as your computer, and
- Have the *iStopCamera app* (free from the *App Store*) open.

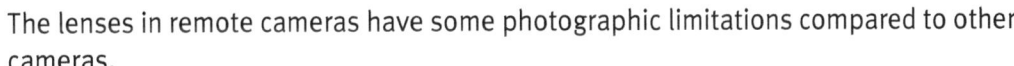

Devices with lower resolution cameras (iPad 2 and iPod Touch) should be used in horizontal position for the best image quality.

One of the benefits of using these cameras is fewer cables across your desk. So make sure your device is fully charged before you start or you will need to connect a charger cable.

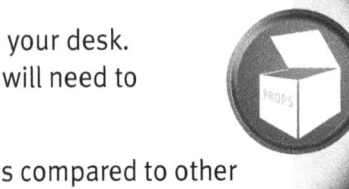

The lenses in remote cameras have some photographic limitations compared to other cameras.

To extend the functionality of the iPhone camera lens, use the Olloclip lens attachment (*www.olloclip.com*). This adds additional views such as: macro, wide angle and fisheye.

Alternatively, you can improve the functions of remote cameras using common magnifying lenses. For example, the iPad 2 and iPod Touch have a fixed focus which means they cannot focus closer than around 30cm. Moving the camera away from the object will eventually bring it into focus, but the object becomes much smaller. This is a problem for getting close ups of small characters such as LEGO® minifigures.

Use a rubber bank to hold a magnifying glass, in this case a small loupe used by stamp and coin collectors, over a remote camera lens for a large crisp close-up.

Get to know the settings on your camera and before you start recording set the exposure and white balance. If possible, lock these settings so they can't automatically change. Constantly changing exposure and white balance can create a flickering effect and ruin your movie.

Exposure

Exposure is the brightness of the picture. If you are recording in a dark place the pictures will be too dark so increase the camera's exposure to brighten the pictures. If you are recording in a bright place, decrease the camera's exposure because the pictures may be too light and washed out.

The exposure on iPad, iPhone and iPod Touch cameras is set directly inside iStopMotion (see *Remote camera settings* on page 117).

White balance

White balance adjusts the 'colour' of the picture. Different types of light sources create slightly different colour shades. Sunlight or daylight produces white whites and a vivid range of natural colours. In comparison, lightbulbs produce a yellowish light and fluorescent tubes produce a blueish light. LED lights are available in the range of white colours. Select a white balance setting which compensates for the lighting you are using and produces a more 'balanced' lighting colour.

However, you could use a particular white balance setting to enhance your story. A campfire might look better if it was a warm cosy yellowish colour, and a ghost story or a laboratory scene might suit a cold blueish colour.

Colour correction

Always make sure your stage has the best room lighting possible and adjust your camera settings before trying to fix the colour in iStopMotion. iStopMotion has a colour correction control (see *Colour correction* on page 116).

The white balance on iPad, iPhone and iPod Touch cameras is set directly inside iStopMotion (see *Remote camera settings* on page 117).

Macro

Every camera lens has a minimum distance at which it can achieve focus. Sometimes this means you can't get the camera close enough and small details, such as LEGO® minifigure faces, remain small on the screen. Attempting to get the camera closer results in a blurry picture.

Use the camera's macro feature, or add a macro or close-up lens. For iPad, iPhone and iPod Touch cameras place a magnifying glass in front of the lens to achieve a much closer picture with focus.

Camera tripod

Good camera tripods are sturdy and heavy so are less prone to being accidentally bumped. They also have a smooth moving fluid head, and usually cost a lot of money.

You can improve the stability of a lightweight tripod by making it heavier. Fill a 2 litre plastic bottle with water and hang it from under the centre of the tripod (shown).

Tripods which allow the camera to be positioned horizontally above the stage are useful for some shots (see *Flat 2D animation* on page 148).

Remote camera mounts

The Viewbase (*www.theinyourface.com/products/viewbase*) is a secure mount for the iPhone and iPod Touch. It clamps onto a firm support whether below, above or to the side of the set. It has a flexible neck and a swivel head which can place the camera right into the set at a wide range of positions.

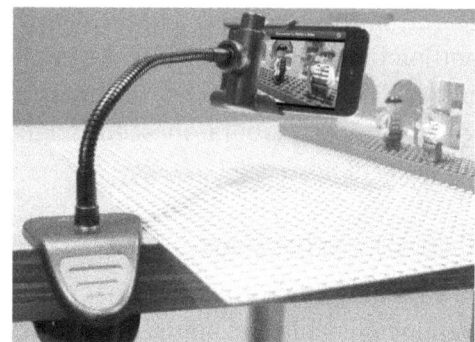

The Stabile Coil Pro (*www.thoughtout.biz/stabile-coil-pro*) is a sturdy stand for the iPad. This stand is very flexible and can position the iPad on any surface up to 45cm off the ground. It has a swivel head to position the iPad at almost any angle. The Grapple accessory also secures the iPad to the stand, increasing the range of positions, even upside down. The Naja King uses a similar design for the iPhone and iPod Touch.

How to make a camera mount

Most cameras have a 1/4" threaded hole in their base for fitting to a tripod or mount.

The simplest form of camera mount is a piece of wood with a hole for a wingnut screw to tighten to the camera. A hardware shop will have wingnuts and may even drill the hole for you.

Cut a small base board out of wood (10-20mm is ideal), with a 1/4" hole in the centre. Secure your camera to the wood with a 1/4" wingnut screw. Be careful not to over tighten. Use washers to pack out the wingnut if necessary.

Use wooden blocks under the back end of the base to give clearance for the head of the wingnut and to angle the camera.

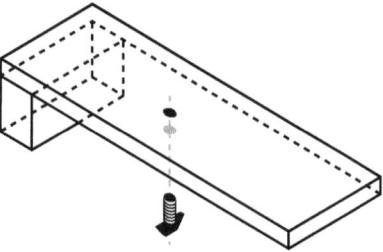

A wooden camera mount can be attached to a vertical support to make a horizontal mount above the stage. Make sure your whole structure is securely screwed or clamped together and well balanced so there is no risk of it falling and damaging your camera or yourself.

The *Logitech HD Pro C920 webcam* has a 1/4"
threaded hole and can be mounted with a
heavy block and a support arm. In this example
the base of the block is 100x100mm and
has a weight of at least 1kg (2.2 pounds) to
counterbalance the camera.

The camera hangs upsidedown from the arm
using a bolt in the threaded hole. iStopMotion
has a setting the orientate the picture the correct way. The arm is
screwed to the base and can be adjusted to a range of heights.

Make the arm from material approximately 20mm x 20mm and drill
1.4" holes both ways through the protruding end to accomodate a
wide range of camera positions.

How to make a remote camera mount

The iPad, iPhone and iPod Touch devices give different
viewpoints when the camera is at the top or the bottom
of the device – always check both viewpoints. Here are
several ways to make your own mounts:

- Achim's DIY Origami iPhone Stand. Download
  a template to make your own from a sheet of
  cardboard (*www.boinx.com/istopmotion/ipad/
  accessories*)

- Make a mount for the iPhone or iPod Touch using
  LEGO® bricks

- For the iPad, you can make a stand out of wood (see
  below left). The iPad can be held at several upright
  angles. The iPad Animation stand (see below right)
  is available from *www.ipadanimation.net/store.html*.

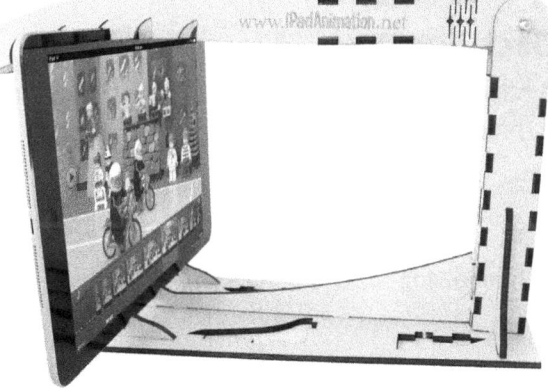

Lighting

Two pictures taken a short time apart may have slightly different lighting. Playing back the series of pictures may look like someone has been switching the light on and off. The reason is that the light from the sun is not constant. Our eyes have learned to make adjustments and we don't notice.

So, while it is easy and cheap to use sunlight for stop motion, if you want **to achieve good lighting you'll need to use artificial lighting.** Look around the room and place your table under the ceiling light so you won't cast shadows on your stage.

One of the **easiest ways to light your set** is to aim a bright light at a white surface above your stage (such as a ceiling or bounce board) so that the light bounces onto your stage. This 'second hand' light gives a soft, even tone with little shadow (see *Bounce board* on page 102).

A **better lighting set up** for stop motion uses a number of small lights and no natural lighting. You'll need to shut the curtains and work in a darkened room.

Key light

The key light has the greatest influence on the look of the scene. Position it at the front of the stage on one side so that your characters are well lit.

Fill light

A fill light is used to reduce shadows created by the key light. Position it at the front of the stage but on the opposite side to the key light. It should not be as bright as the key light, so use a lower wattage bulb, move the light further away or use a diffuser (see *Diffuser* on page 101).

Back light

A back light helps separate characters from the background and gives them a three-dimensional look.

Place a back light behind the stage to light the props and characters from behind. Take care not to get glare into the camera lens.

The following picture shows a typical stage set with lights:

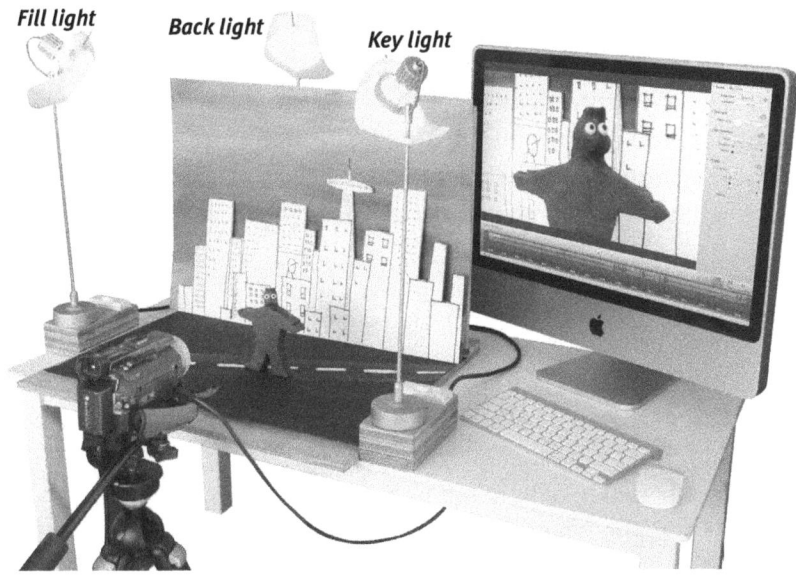

The combination of lights placed in the right position, with the correct brightness, will create an excellent effect. Desk lamps with flexible stands work well for small sets. You can use different wattage bulbs to create the right effect. Use 'flood' type bulbs with the widest spread, eg 60°, for the softest light. 'Spot' lights have a narrower beam, eg 36°, and give stronger light but create more shadows.

LED bulbs are expensive, but use very little power and are safer to work with as they don't create as much heat. You may need a diffuser to soften the light.

If you feel your stage is not bright enough, move the lights closer, use a higher wattage light bulb, add an extra light or check the exposure settings on your camera.

Soft, even lighting

Test your lighting by taking some test pictures in iStopMotion. Are the colours bright and true? If there are reflections and white patches, your light is probably too bright. Move the light further away, use a smaller wattage lightbulb, a dimmer, a diffuser or a bounce board to spread the light more evenly.

Diffuser

A diffuser is semi opaque material placed in front of a bulb to soften the effect of light. There are many ways to make your own, eg greaseproof paper, as long as it is not so close to the bulb that it catches fire. Big screen movies use a sheet of special heat resistant gel. Contact an event lighting company to buy a small piece of diffuser gel.

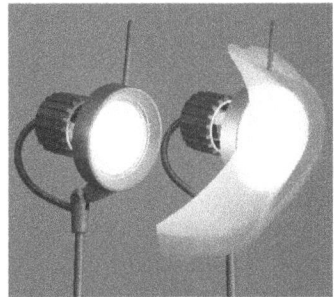

Bounce board

Use white card or foamboard to bounce light onto your stage. Foamboard is a rigid lightweight sheet with a smooth white surface. You can buy it from art supply shops. Contact a signwriter or digital colour bureau to get offcut or slightly damaged pieces of foamboard cheaply.

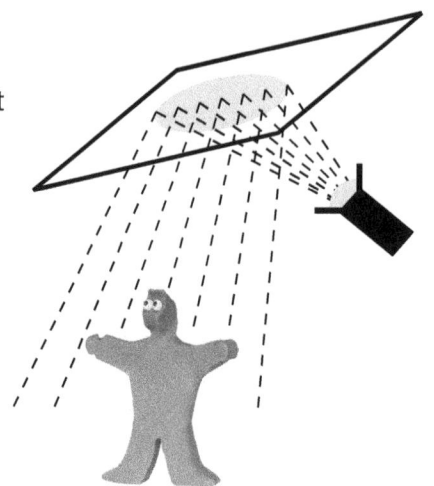

Bounce boards don't need to be very big. To cast light onto the faces of your characters, place a small piece of white paper on the stage in front of the character (out of sight of the camera) to bounce ambient room light onto the character. In the following picture, the main source of light on the characters is from the right. The left side of the picture is darker and the characters are in shadow.

In the second picture a small piece of white paper has been added to 'bounce' the main light back onto the left side of the characters. The paper would usually be out of sight of the camera, but is shown here to demonstrate the effect. Using 'second hand' light is a safe, cheap and effective way to increase the amount of light on the set.

Clothing can reflect unwanted colour and random light onto your stage. Wear plain dark clothes for the least reflection.

Small lights such as clip on reading lights or mobile phones can be useful to make some areas of the set brighter than other areas.

Lighting for dramatic effect

Use the position of lights to create dramatic effects in your movies. In most cases, the lighting effects will be more effective when matched with the soundtrack.

Here are some other ideas for using lights:
- Putting a front spotlight very low will give your character a 'larger than life' shadow on the wall behind them
- Putting a light directly above the character will produce ominous shadows on their faces
- If your soundtrack has lightning, shine a bright light on the set for one picture, then darken the set by covering it with a sheet of card for one picture. Repeat this sequence with less intensity
- Simulate the passage of time, eg a day, in a few seconds by slowly moving a light across the set allowing shadows and reflections to provide the animation
- In a scary movie, quickly shine a spotlight across the set to indicate an ominous presence. This is more effective if the light is partially obscured behind walls and reflected through windows. Create hidden areas for the character and the threatening presence to hide from each other
- Shine a small LED light through translucent items to create natural looking flickering effects.

Safety note

Remember lights get hot – make sure they don't melt your set or burn your fingers. Take care not to touch lights, even when warm, because bulbs are fragile and expensive.

Always make sure your stage area is safe to work around. Electrical cables from lights, cameras and computers can be dangerous.

Take the time to run cables behind your stage and under your table so there is no risk of tripping.

Use duct tape to secure cables on the floor in walking areas.

How to make a portable stage

In an ideal world, you would have a special area where you could leave your stop motion stage set up until your stop motion is finished. But sometimes you'll need to pack away your stage because the space is needed for something else. For this reason, it is a good idea to use a portable stage that can easily be moved.

The stage can be any size, but if you plan to use LEGO® a logical size is to accommodate 6 base plates (25.5cm square). This is how to make your own portable stage.

You'll need three pieces of plywood (12mm or similar):
- **base** – 77cm x 56cm
- **back** – 77cm x 40cm
- **strip** – 77cm x 5cm.

And from thicker wood – two **braces** shaped from 250mm tall x 50mm wide.

Step 1

Position the braces behind the back (15cm in from each side) and fix together with glue and 50mm screws.

Step 2

Position the strip on top of one long edge of the base and fix the two pieces together with glue and 20mm screws.

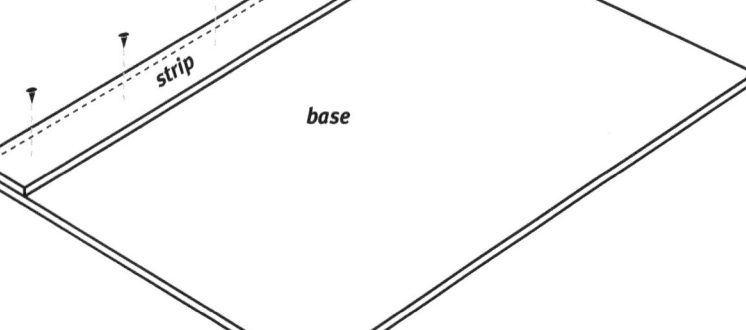

Step 3

Position the back on top of the base and join together with two hinges and short (max 12mm) screws.

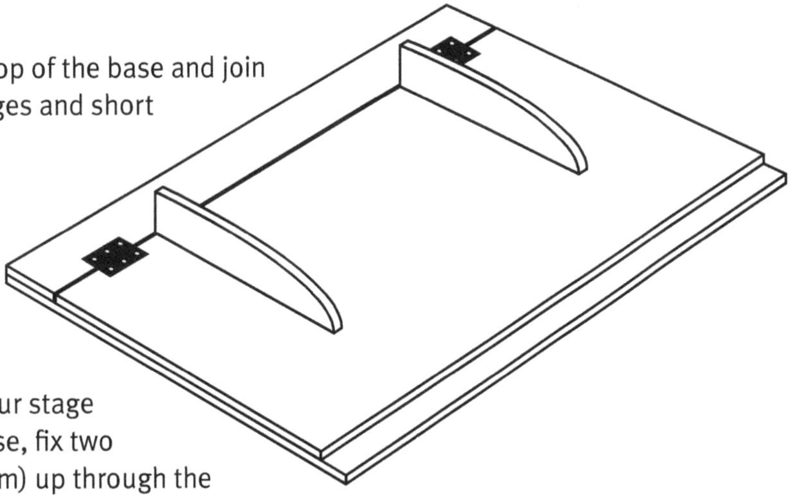

Step 4

Lift the back to reveal your stage. To hold your stage firmly open when in use, fix two long screws (min 60mm) up through the base and into the back braces (shown). Simply remove these two screws with a screwdriver when you want to pack down your stage.

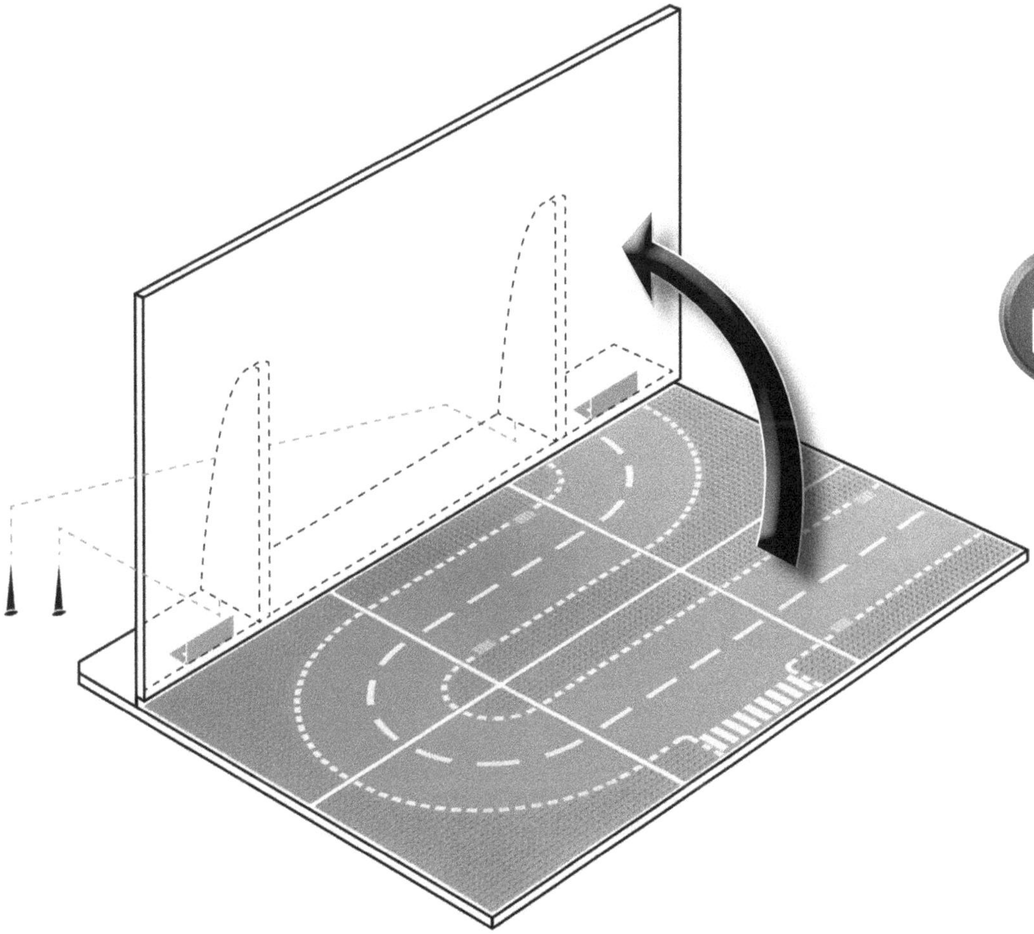

Pictures

Instant gratification with stop motion

The traditional task of editing raw movie footage doesn't exist with stop motion. *Each picture is assessed when recorded and if it is not suitable a replacement picture is recorded. At any point in the process, all pictures should be final. So when the last picture is taken the movie is complete. Where editing is required, the iStopMotion movie can be opened in iMovie, but this may only be for tasks such as adding a title or credits.*

In this chapter you will record the pictures for your stop motion. You will learn about:

- iStopMotion software
- Recording the pictures
- Making a LEGO® minifigure walk
- Making a character talk
- Creating visual effects and recording action sequences
- Avoiding common stop motion mistakes
- Adding a soundtrack
- Adding a background
- Saving your stop motion.

Our website (*stop-motion-handbook.com*) has a link to buy iStopMotion. Or for more information about software features go to *www.boinx.com*

> **Checklist before recording the pictures**
> ☐ Soundtrack is complete
> ☐ Tape down all backgrounds, artwork and LEGO® base boards, so they can't accidentally move
> ☐ Control all lighting sources, including blocking windows, using appropriate artificial lights with diffusers and bounce boards
> ☐ Clear working area and secure tripod to avoid accidental movement.

iStopMotion

Open iStopMotion, then select File⤳New to create a new stop motion.

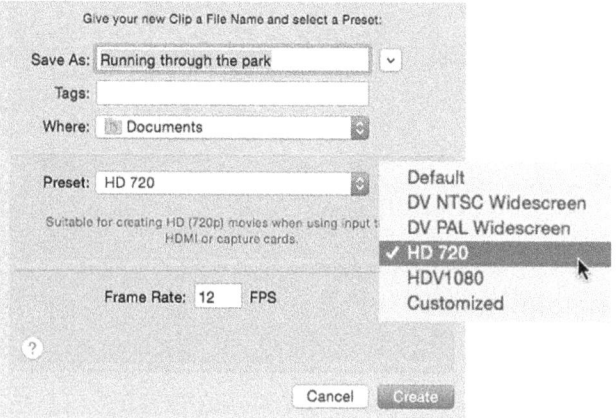

There are two important settings required to record a new stop motion:

Picture size (Preset)

Presets are settings for the picture sizes of different types of movies. You may see a different list as it can be customised (iStopMotion menu⤳Preferences) to show only the types of movies you want.

Select a preset which is the maximum picture size you are likely to need, and that your camera can produce.

iStopMotion has a range of presets including:

- Default – 960 x 540 pixels, a good general purpose resolution. It is a useful size for movies on the iPhone, iPad and Apple TV and can easily be reduced for other uses such as DVD or internet

- DV PAL Widescreen – 720 x 576 pixels (plays as 16:9 to suit wide screens) suitable for DVDs. (Choose DV NTSC 720 x 480 pixels for North American DVDs). Don't confuse this wide shape with 'high definition' because it is the same file size as standard definition DV PAL, but uses rectangular pixels to simulate a wider picture shape
- HD 720 – 1280 x 720 pixels suitable for the smallest of the high definition standards. The larger size HD 1080 is also available
- The Customised preset allows you to create a picture size, for a specific unique purpose, up to a very large 8192 pixels x 8192 pixels.

Picture rate (Frame rate)

The secret to making something come to life in pictures is the speed you 'flip' through the pictures. Movie makers have worked out that around 25 pictures per second* (also called 'frame rate', or 'FPS') give believable movement. That is 25 pictures for every second of your stop motion. When recording a video, the camera does this automatically for you. However, in stop motion you need to record every one of those 25 pictures one at a time.

> 1 second = 25 pictures
> 1 minute = 1500 pictures
> 1 hour = 90,000 pictures

The big screen movie *Chicken Run* is 82 minutes long, plus DVD menus and bonus features. At least 123,000 pictures needed to be recorded – one at a time! The filmmaker's goal was to record 10 seconds of the movie each day.

Picture rate is one factor which will determine how smooth or jumpy your stop motion animation will be, and how long it will take you to make it.

* *PAL TV format uses 25FPS, NTSC TV format uses 30FPS. Cinema movies use 24FPS. Peter Jackson's Hobbit movies used a higher picture rate of 48FPS. Movies created specifically for the internet such as YouTube use 30FPS.*

How many pictures do I need for animation?

Choosing the picture rate for your stop motion is often a balance between how much time you have and the quality you want. Reduce the number of pictures per second and it won't take as long to make the stop motion. Reduce the picture rate too much and it will make a jumpy animation.

If you need to create an ambitious multi-media project, iStopMotion can create stop motion up to 100 FPS.

> When learning to make stop motion, or if you don't have much time, use **6 FPS**.
>
> In most situations, use **10-15 FPS** for good quality animation.
>
> For high quality movies use **30 FPS**.

1-8 FPS

Very low picture rates are suitable when you have a short time to record the stop motion or the subject matter suits a more 'jumpy' result. At 1 FPS, a one minute stop motion will have just 60 pictures.

These low picture rates work well for:

- slideshows (1 FPS)
- animated artistic works such as painting and sculpture (2-8 FPS)
- stories told with a graphic medium, such as paper cutout characters, where realistic animation is not required (6 FPS)
- first ever stop motion when you are learning (6 FPS).

10, 12 or 15 FPS

Above 10 pictures per second, the eye perceives fluid motion between pictures and good animation results can be produced.

These picture rates are half the 'full speed'. We use 12 FPS in many of the examples in this book.

These halve the time required to record a high quality stop motion and are suitable for almost any situation where realistic animation movements are required, including stories using LEGO® or Plasticine characters.

At 12 FPS, a one minute stop motion will have 720 pictures.

25 or 30 FPS

We'll call these high picture rates 'full speed', because this is the number of pictures in big screen movies.

These high picture rates can produce very high quality animation as long as all other areas of production, such as lighting, character design and story are also high quality.

At 25 FPS, every minute of stop motion will have 1500 pictures.

Changing the picture rate after the stop motion is made

The picture rate is fundamental to the stop motion. It was the first setting entered before the stop motion was made and cannot be changed directly. However, if after recording pictures you decide they would look better if they went faster or slower, here is a method which allows you to use a different the picture rate:

- Select all frames in the stop motion (CMD-A)
- Select File⇢Export Selection⇢As Images
- Open a new iStopMotion file with the required picture rate and the same picture size
- Select Movie⇢Import Images⇢from Disk…

How do picture rates affect character movements?

Moving your characters bit by bit usually works really well, but sometimes, to get the timing just right, it can help to know a little about the maths involved.

Regardless of the picture rate, you want character movements at a realistic speed. For example, if you want the character to move across the screen in 5 seconds:

- 1 FPS will mean very large movements between pictures (eg 5cm)
- 12 FPS means more pictures and smaller movements (eg 5mm)
- 25 FPS means many more pictures and very small movements (eg 2mm).

In this example, 15 pictures are needed to move the character on the left closer to the one on the right (Jim) before the dialogue. Generally, it looks more natural for characters to move in curved paths rather than straight lines (see *Principles of animation* on page 164).

Time lapse

Time lapse is a special type of stop motion. It condenses a long process into a short stop motion movie. Use time lapse for events such as the moon rising, a butterfly hatching, a scientific reaction, a study of traffic on the road, an ice block melting or as a security camera (see *Time lapse* on page 150).

To record an **event** with time lapse you need to work out how many pictures are required. Because the computer is taking the pictures automatically there is no extra work for you so use the full speed picture rate of 25 (or 30) pictures per second:

Pictures in movie	= Movie duration required (in seconds) x 25 pictures per second

For example, to produce a stop motion that was 8 minutes long (480 seconds) at 25 pictures per second, you'd need 12,000 pictures.

Then you need to work out how frequently to capture each of those pictures.

Picture capture rate	= Total recording time (in seconds) / pictures required in movie

If the event lasted 9 hours (32,400 seconds) and you needed 12,000 pictures, you need to record one picture every 2.7 seconds.

This is the figure used for the Time lapse interval (see *Time lapse* on page 150). Once you've set up your computer and camera to record the pictures, you can leave it to do the job, in this case, for 9 hours.

You can also use time lapse for **individual scenes** of a story based stop motion, as appropriate – it all depends on the nature of the animation movements. Use time lapse as a tool to assist. Having the time lapse clock ticking may be put some pressure on you, so select a suitable interval. Almost certainly it will help you finish your movie more quickly.

If a scene requires a car to drive across the screen, estimate how long it will take you to move your hands to the set, move the car and withdraw your hands – this is the interval (say 6 seconds). Set time lapse recording and record as many pictures as you need for that scene.

The iStopMotion window

The iStopMotion window has all the controls you need to make your stop motion.

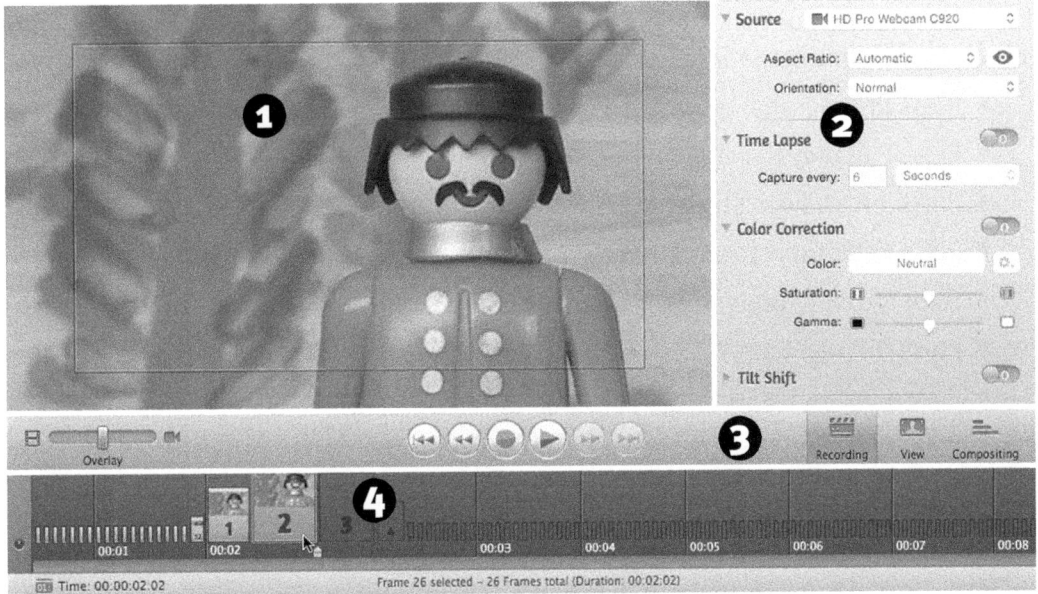

❶ Preview Area

The Preview Area shows the view from your camera, the last recorded picture or a transparent combination of both, depending on the setting of the **Overlay** slider in the Toolbar ❸:

- Press OPT-1 (or drag the Overlay slider to the left) to show the **recorded picture**
- Press OPT-2 shows a combined image of both the last recorded picture, and the current camera view. This is the normal view when recording pictures – the difference between the two images appears as a ghosted image providing helpful feedback on the parts that have been animated. See also *Onion skinning* on page 127
- Press OPT-3 (or drag the Overlay slider to the right) to show the **camera view.**

❷ Sidebar

The Sidebar displays panes of options to assist making stop motion:

- Press CMD-1 to show/hide the **Recording pane**
- Press CMD-2 to show/hide the **View pane**
- Press CMD-3 to show/hide the **Compositing pane.**

❸ Toolbar

At the left end of the Toolbar is the Overlay slider (see Preview Area ❶). The Toolbar also has transport controls for recording and playing the stop motion, and buttons for switching the pane in the Sidebar ❷:

- Press the spacebar to **record** a picture
- Press P to **play** the stop motion
- Press left arrow to show the **previous picture**
- Press right arrow to show the **next picture**
- Press OPT-left arrow to skip **backward one second**
- Press OPT-right arrow to skip **forward one second**
- Press CMD-Home to show the **first picture**
- Press CMD-End to show the **last recorded picture**.

❹ Timeline

The lower part of the iStopMotion window contains the Timeline that shows thumbnails of the pictures taken. The playhead highlights the current picture. The Timeline can also display soundtrack files and reference videos. The status bar under the Timeline has information about your stop motion movie.

> ### Storyboard
>
> *On big screen movies is it usual to develop the script into a storyboard. A storyboard adds illustrations to the script to communicate to everyone making the movie what the pictures should look like.*
>
> *Creating a storyboard is a good idea to demonstrate understanding of the script and helps with planning the movie production, finding the right locations, making the right props etc.*
>
> *For short stop motion movies it is feasible to skip the storyboard and decide the best camera angle at the start of each scene.*

Making a stop motion

Here is an overview of the process to record the pictures for a stop motion movie.

Step 1: Opening iStopMotion
- Open iStopMotion and select 'File⋯>New'

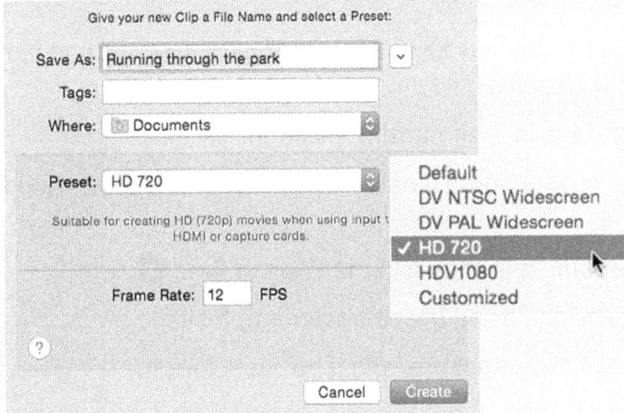

- Enter the name for your stop motion
- From the popup menu labelled 'Where', select a folder to save your stop motion. By default this will be your 'Movies' folder. If you have created a project folder save the iStopMotion file into it
- Select the Preset for the type of pictures you want for your stop motion, eg HD 720
- Enter the Frame Rate for the number of pictures you want to record for each second (see *Picture rate* on page 109)
- Click the Create button to save the iStopMotion file.

You are ready to make your stop motion.

Autosave
Make sure the Autosave feature is turned on (iStopMotion menu ⋯>Preferences) so that in the unlikely event of an computer crash or a power cut, your file will be safe. On the Preferences General panel specify how often you want to autosave, eg after every 5 pictures. Depending on the speed of your computer, autosaving may cause a slight delay in recording pictures.

Every time you complete a scene or want to watch the stop motion, select File⋯>Save (CMD-S) to make sure all pictures are saved.

Step 2: Choosing the camera

- Make sure your camera (video camera, webcam or DSLR) is turned on and connected to the computer.

  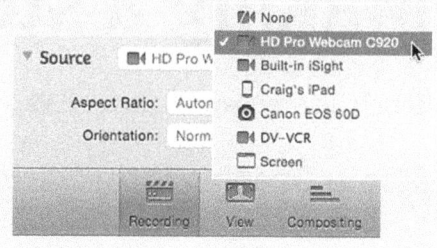

  If you are using a remote camera (iPad, iPhone or iPod Touch) open the iStopCamera app (free from the *App Store*). You will need to accept the connection on the device

- Click the Recording button on the Toolbar ❸ (CMD-1) to show the Recording pane. On the Source panel choose the camera
- Put your characters onto the stage in their starting position
- Position your camera and make sure your characters have room to move around in that scene
- Check that the view from the camera is shown in the Preview Area ❶
- Set the camera to **manual focus** and bring the character into focus
- Set the camera's **white balance** and **exposure**, and if possible lock it.

If your video camera automatically turns off after a short time when on battery power, try plugging the camera into a power outlet and removing any tapes from the camera.

Colour Correction

Before adjusting the colour in iStopMotion, make sure the room lighting conditions are the best you can achieve (see *Lighting* on page 100). Then, if the picture colour is still not what you want:

- Check the exposure and white balance settings on the camera (see *Exposure* on page 96)
- Turn on Colour Correction in the Recording pane:
  - To change the overall colour cast (**tint**) – click the word next to 'Color' and on the colour wheel move the black dot in the direction of the colour that you want. To save this colour, click the button.
  - To change the colour **saturation** – move the slider right to make the colours more saturated or move it left to dilute the colours. Move the slider all the way to the left to make the picture black and white

116

- To change the brightness (**gamma**) – move the slider right to make the picture brighter or move it left to make the picture darker.

Changing the Colour Correction does not affect the pictures already recorded. But if you did want to change existing pictures, select the thumbnails and export them (File⋯⟩Export Selection⋯⟩As Images). Set the colour correction to the required colour. Reimport the images (Movie⋯⟩Import Images⋯⟩from Disk) and the colour correction will be applied.

To reset the Colour Correction settings (does not affect the pictures already recorded), click the button and select 'Default'.

If, after making your stop motion, you're not happy with the colour, it can be further adjusted in iMovie (see *Adjusting the clip* on page 178).

Remote camera settings

Click the Configure button (these settings can be made in the Preview Area ❶ or on the device screen):

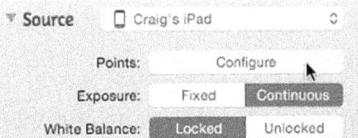

Exposure

If the picture is too light or too dark, drag the circle exposure icon to the part of the picture that has the right brightness.

- If you want the lighting to change with the lighting conditions, select 'Continuous' in the sidebar. This means that if the lighting gets darker the picture will darken

- If you want the lighting to remain at the same level, select 'Fixed'. This means that if the lighting gets darker the camera will automatically adjust to brighten the picture.

White Balance

If in the overall colour of the picture whites are not white due to room lighting, set the white balance:

- Make sure White Balance is set to 'Unlocked'
- Hold a sheet of white paper in front of your camera
- Wait a couple of seconds for the camera to adjust the colour to this new white
- Select White Balance to 'Locked' to store this new white.

Focus

The back cameras of the iPhone 4 and later, and the 3rd gen iPad and later, have a manual focus setting. Tap Focus in the top left of the device screen and drag the square graphic onto the part of the picture you want in focus – often the speaking character's face. Reset the focus every time you move the camera.

Step 3: Importing soundtrack

Click the View button (CMD-2) on the Toolbar to show the View pane. On the Soundtrack panel click the button ✣ to import the soundtrack. The file can be in a range of common audio formats, including MP3, AIFF, WAV and CAF. You can also import a movie and only its soundtrack will be used. The green waveform for the soundtrack appears above the thumbnail pictures in the Timeline.

Interpreting the soundtrack waveform

The waveform lets you 'see' your sound. Click and hold on the waveform and the soundtrack will play so you can hear what is coming up.

Always aim to match character actions with the distinct parts of the soundtrack and plan your character movements to achieve this. Accurately matching your pictures with your sound is an easy way to make your movie powerful.

You only need to consider one scene ahead. Hold the cursor over the Timeline for a magnified view to count the number of pictures required to match a specific point in the soundtrack. Use the beat of music and other sounds to add power to the pictures by changing the camera view on that frame.

In this case the soundtrack starts quiet. At 2.5 seconds a small sound starts. This is likely to be a good place to show the title so don't start animating the story yet. You need an opening image which will lead to introducing a character for the first spoken dialogue just after 6 seconds.

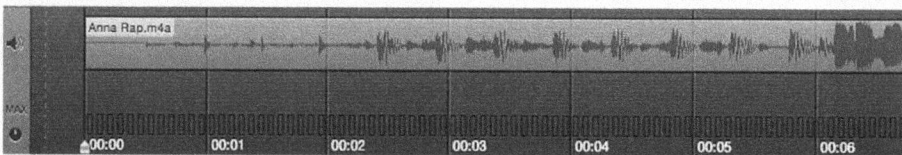

Within a block of dialogue, look for flatter lines which may indicate a breath and therefore may require smaller animation movements compared to speaking movements.

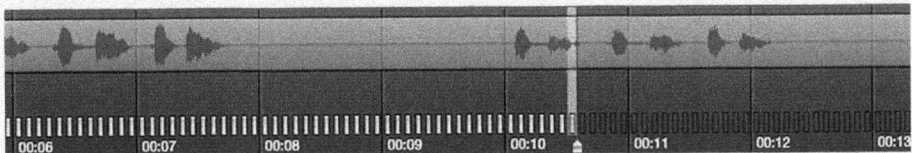

- To start the soundtrack later (for example, if you need to add pictures for the introduction or title sequence before the soundtrack starts) move the soundtrack to the right. Specify an **offset** in hours, minutes, seconds and frames, eg 00:00:12:18 to add 12 seconds and 18 frames of silence at the start

- To start the soundtrack part way through (for example, if there is silence at the start) move the soundtrack to the left. Specify a **negative offset** in hours, minutes, seconds and frames, eg –00:00:03:10 to skip the first 3 seconds and 10 frames

Breaking a soundtrack into sections

If you want to have several groups recording pictures for the stop motion at the same time (big screen movies call them 'units') you'll need to give each group the appropriate part of the soundtrack. Listen to the soundtrack and note the time (minutes and seconds) for the start of each section, and also how long each section is.

For each group import the full original soundtrack, and use a negative offset to adjust the start of the soundtrack. Advise each group how long their section is.

Afterwards save each stop motion section and join them together in iMovie, matching the pictures to the full original soundtrack. If groups record a few seconds more pictures than required you'll be able to use transitions to join the sections.

Step 4: Recording your first picture

There are two ways to record stop motion pictures:

- **Single frames** – records ONE picture every time you press the spacebar or click the red Record button on the Toolbar.

  Capture more than one copy of the same picture with these keyboard shortcuts:

  - Two pictures   press 2
  - Three pictures   press 3
  - Four pictures   press 4

  Don't overuse this time-saving technique as you will end up with a slide show rather than an animation

- **Time lapse** – automatically record one picture every 'x' seconds, minutes or hours – whatever you specify (see pages 112 and 150).

  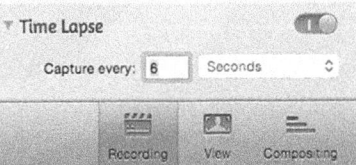

Animation process

Recording pictures is a simple task with two parts:
- animate (move) the character, and
- record the picture.

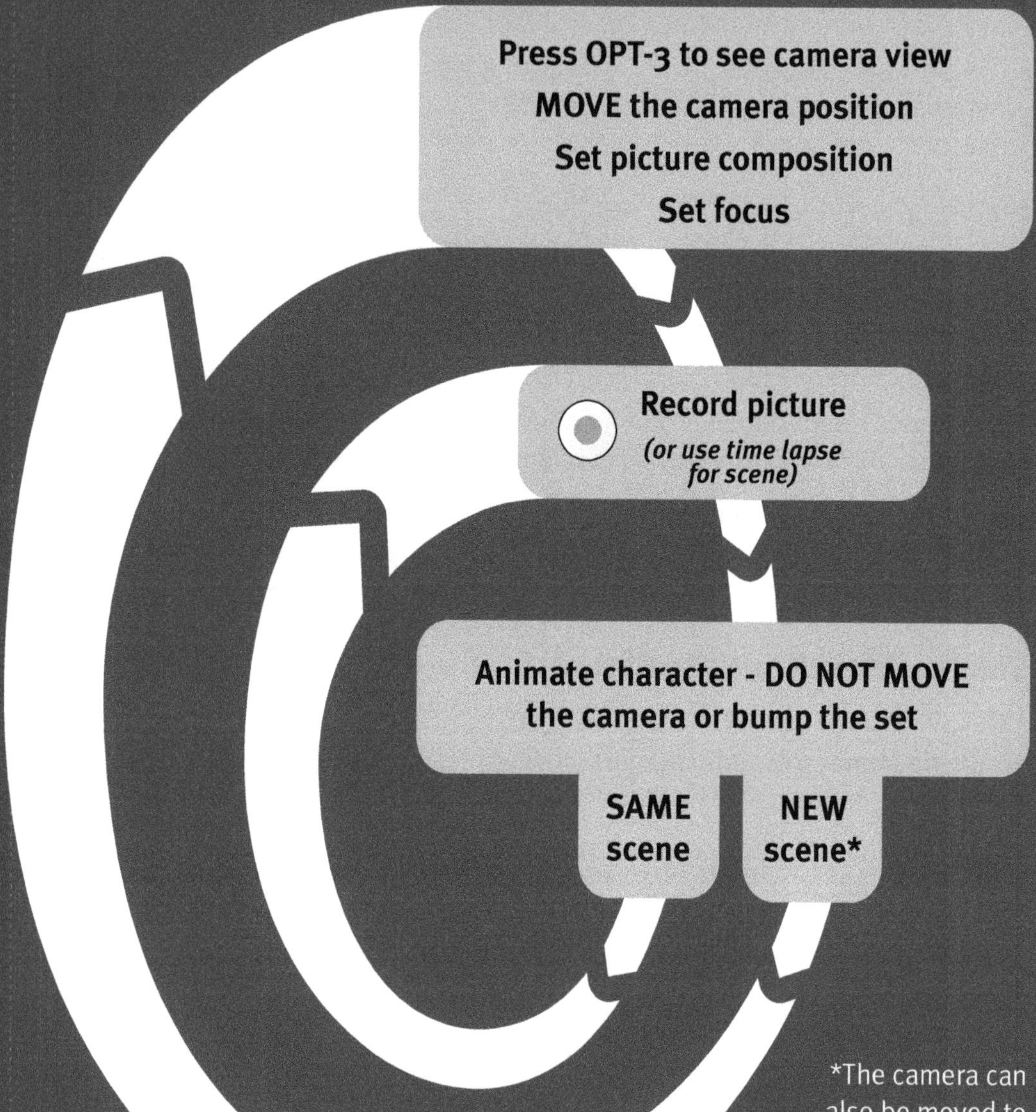

Press OPT-3 to see camera view
MOVE the camera position
Set picture composition
Set focus

Record picture
(or use time lapse for scene)

Animate character - DO NOT MOVE the camera or bump the set

SAME scene   **NEW scene***

*The camera can also be moved to a new position in the middle of a scene to add tension or to hide the result of the camera being bumped.

Some **digital still cameras** are able to display a live preview to the computer - click the button 📷.

Other **digital still cameras** are not able to display a live preview so iStopMotion displays a second record button in the transport controls. Click the left Preview button to show the view from the camera. Click the right Record button to capture the picture.

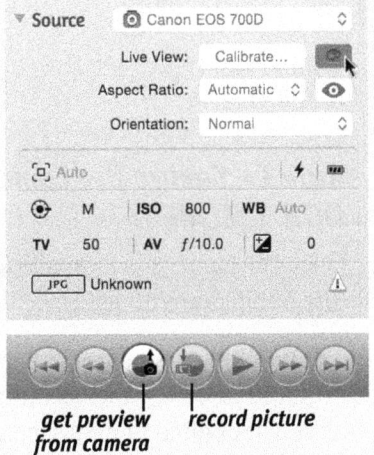

get preview from camera   *record picture*

Title

The decision about where and how the title will be displayed should be made when creating the soundtrack (see *Audio for title and credits* on page 46). The title doesn't have to appear first. In some cases it may be more appropriate to show the title after the first scene.

The title can be animated in iStopMotion or can be added in iMovie afterwards as an editing task (see *Adding titles* on page 172).

The title can be a static image, such as the name of the movie illustrated on paper, or you could animate it, building it in LEGO® or some other creative idea. Display the title for at least 3 seconds (36 pictures) so the audience has time to read it.

If you want to use one of the high quality title options in iMovie, put the lens cap on the camera and record black pictures until the first scene starts. Another good option is to record several seconds of a blurry or bland pictures to add the title over. If you want to display the title over an introductory animation scene, such as a car driving in, keep important details away from the centre of the screen where the title will appear.

Step 5: Bringing your characters to life

Viewing lots of pictures in a rapid fashion will result in a smooth motion to the human eye – the idea behind stop motion. So, to bring your characters to life:

- Move the characters only a small amount
- Press the spacebar to record a picture. The picture is added into the Timeline as a thumbnail to the right of the playhead. The playhead automatically marks the new picture with a blue highlight to show where the next picture will be added
- Repeat these two steps until you have captured a complete action or movement, or your whole stop motion.

If you captured a picture you don't like, or someone's hand got in the way – delete it. Select the thumbnail in the Timeline and press CMD-delete.

For the best results, keep the camera position fixed for each scene. Do whatever you can to make sure the camera does not get bumped (see *Rule 1* on page 122).

Important rules

Of all the tips to make better quality stop motion, these two rules will make the most difference.

Rule 1 – Secure the camera on a tripod/mount and DON'T MOVE IT

Once the camera is in position, move only the characters for that scene, line of dialogue or action.

The number of pictures in a sequence will depend on the actions required to match the soundtrack. Unless you are recording a high action sequence or a music video, moving the camera before 12 pictures (one second) will usually be a mistake.

Music videos often have very fast image sequences requiring several camera angles per second.

Unless you have a very high quality tripod, trying to move the camera every picture may destroy your movie because the result may be very jumpy, confusing and hard to watch. In some cases, you may be able to achieve a movement effect by sliding the stage and keeping the camera steady, or placing the camera and stand on a sliding platform.

Rule 2 – MOVE the camera to a new and very different angle for a new scene, line of dialogue or action.

Each camera move should help the audience follow the story and become more engaged in the action. You might start off with a wide shot of the whole scene and then a series of close-ups as each character says their lines (see *How to dramatise an action sequence* on page 143). For a natural look, the camera angle needs to move at least 30°. Moving the camera just a little to a slightly different position will look like a mistake.

When setting a new camera angle, consider all possibilities, such as:

- Moving the camera and tripod/mount
- Moving the stage
- Moving the character to a new part of the background.

When resetting the camera position, move the Overlay slider to the right (OPT-3) to show the camera view without any ghosting of the recorded picture.

If it does get bumped, delete the picture (CMD-Delete). Then start the sequence again, or to make it look like you did it on purpose, move the camera to a completely new position for the rest of the scene (see *Rule 2* on page 122).

The camera settings in the Source panel can be changed as you make your stop motion. For example, if the character needs to walk on the ceiling, rather than trying to suspend the character upside down, it may be easier to set the Orientation to 'Rotated by 180°' and have them walk the right way up. On a remote camera use orientation lock to rotate the picture.

Credits

Make sure you have recorded enough pictures to reach the end of the green waveform (see *Audio for title and credits* on page 46), otherwise the audio will cut off abruptly at the last picture. The last part of the soundtrack is probably for the credits so the pictures do not need animated detail although they could be a closing scene. Or put the lens cap on the camera and finish your movie by recording black pictures. Effects such as fade out can be added in iMovie.

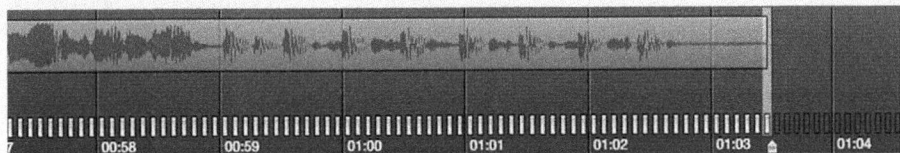

Credits can be recorded in iStopMotion with pictures of a printed artwork or collage design, or you could animate them. Display each screen of credits for at least 3 seconds (36 pictures) so the audience has time to read them.

You can also use the high quality options in iMovie such as scrolling credits (see *Adding titles* on page 172).

Step 6: Playing your stop motion

When you have recorded enough pictures or are ready to watch your work, **first save your stop motion** – File ⟶ Save (CMD-S). Then, either:

- Press P, or click the play button and watch in the Preview Area, or
- Press CMD-SHIFT-F to watch your stop motion in full screen mode.

After you have watched your stop motion, take care to put the playhead back to where you want to record the next picture or they will be added out of order. Move the playhead by clicking on a thumbnail picture so that it is highlighted.

Continues with Step 7 on page 126.

Animation example: Scary Sea

This page shows images of the camera views and character actions for a stop motion called *'Scary Sea'* created by Holly (9) and Emily (12). View the stop motion at www.acumen.net.nz/pages/NMSScarySea.html.

Bland image over which to add the title later.

Camera view from shore, as characters get on boat.

Camera view from boat.

Overhead camera view of whole scene.

Camera view looking up at boat.

Camera view from boat, as shark circles.

Camera view looking up at boat.

Swimming to shark.

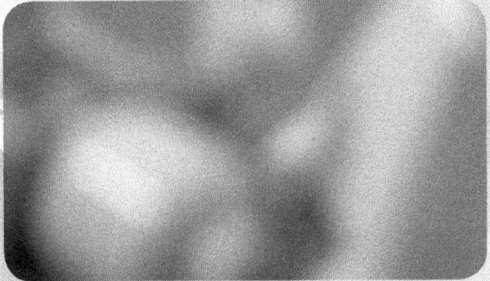

Sequence of random blurry images to convey action.

Camera view down in the water.

Overhead camera view of whole scene.

Safely back on boat and sail away.

Bland image over which to add the credits later.

*We don't condone killing sharks. This was an accidental outcome of the attempt to chase the shark away.

Step 7: Editing your stop motion

When you have recorded all the pictures, review your work:

- Press CMD-Home to go to the first picture at the start of the Timeline
- Press OPT-1 to view the recorded picture (and turn off the camera)
- Press the right arrow button and carefully watch the animation pictures, looking for any areas that need to be fixed, such as:
  - Hands in shot
  - Extra strong lighting, or shadows
  - Quick picture changes that just don't work
  - Bumped camera position.

> To **delete** a picture select the thumbnail (*it highlights blue*) on the Timeline and press CMD-Delete. To restore the match between pictures and sound you'll need to find a nearby place to duplicate a picture
>
> To **duplicate** a picture select a thumbnail, press CMD-C then CMD-V
>
> To **move** a picture select the thumbnail, or hold Shift and click to select a range of thumbnails. Drag them to a new position on the Timeline
>
> To **reverse** the order of a series of pictures Shift-click to select a range of thumbnails. Select Edit⇢Reverse Order.

If you need to edit the soundtrack see *Editing the soundtrack later* on page 71.

Step 8: Saving your stop motion

Select File⇢Save. **This is your master file – don't lose it.**

The iStopMotion file is a Quicktime movie with very high quality. It has a big file size because it is a series of individual pictures rather than in video format. Many computers are unable to play these movies because the files are too big. This is why iStopMotion creates a 'rendered' movie before it can play.

If your next step is editing your stop motion in iMovie, close iStopMotion and open iMovie (see *Editing stop motion clip to make a movie* on page 171). iMovie can open the big iStopMotion file and will compress it after the editing is done.

If your movie is complete in iStopMotion, you'll need to export it as a smaller file to play smoothly. Select File⇢Export to compress the movie to normal video quality. Select the picture size which matches the preset from step 1, eg HD 720. You can also save versions of the stop motion customised for the internet and digital devices.

View options

The View pane has settings for the iStopMotion screen. Click the View button on the Toolbar (CMD-2). These are some of the most useful features:

Grid
Adjust the columns and rows to display guides such as for rules of thirds. The guides are not saved in the stop motion movie.

Overlay (Action safe)
Click the button ✲, and select Action safe.

Action safe is a guide to keep your characters away from the edge of the screen – keep this on at all times. The guide will assist with better picture composition. Text and titles should be within the Title safe guide. The guides are not saved in the movie.

Onion Skinning
Adds further power to the Overlay slider. You can choose to see ghosted impressions of up to 5 previous views. This is could be useful when you need to move your character the same distance every picture.

Rotoscope/Lip-Sync
You can load a video of an action or body movement, and picture by picture, you can view this reference video to assist making realistic body or mouth movements for your characters (see *Importing a reference video* on page 128). The video is not saved in the movie.

Soundtrack
Load a soundtrack into your movie and view the waveform to locate distinctive points such as beats and silences to help synchronise the pictures to the audio (see *Importing soundtrack* on page 118). The soundtrack can be saved as part of the movie.

Importing a reference video

When you want to get a realistic match between the movements of a character and a real life action (such as lip synced mouth shapes, running, jumping, dancing, a combat fight or the walk of an animal) import a video of that action or speech as a reference.

In the Rotoscope/Lip-Sync panel (View pane) click the button to import the video you want to use as a reference. A filmstrip of the video appears in the Timeline above the thumbnail pictures.

Click the Configure button to select whether to view the video in a separate window, or as a ghosted image in the main window.

The video is shown one picture at a time so you can animate your character's mouth or body to match the correct position. The resulting animation will have very natural movement.

Click and hold on the filmstrip and the next portion of the reference video will play so you can see and hear what is coming up. If the video has audio, hover your mouse over the filmstrip and the waveform of the audio is displayed so you can locate distinctive points such as beats and silences.

If the video is a reference for a particular part of the stop motion, use the offset to align the video to the start of that scene. You can only have one reference video at a time. Import as many short videos as you need reference for different actions.

- If you need to move the video left, to align the action with the stop motion, specify a **negative offset** in hours, minutes, seconds and frames, eg –00:00:02:20. This will skip the first 2 seconds and 20 frames of the video

- If you need to move the video right, to align the action with the stop motion, specify an **offset** in hours, minutes, seconds and frames, eg 00:00:11:02. This will start the video after 11 seconds and 2 frames of the stop motion.

Reference videos can be for specific actions or scenes. You don't need to portray the entire stop motion in a video.

When the Playback checkbox is ticked, the soundtrack of the reference video will be saved in your movie. The pictures from the reference video are not included in your stop motion.

If the reference video contains dialogue, you may want this to be part of the final movie. Make sure you record reference videos with good quality audio so it can be used in the final movie (see *Audio chapter* starting on page 33).

But first, let me take a selfie
by Daniel Oliva Andersson

Daniel took one selfie every day for 7 years and put them together in a stop motion.
www.youtube.com/watch?v=sOXSandEa4s

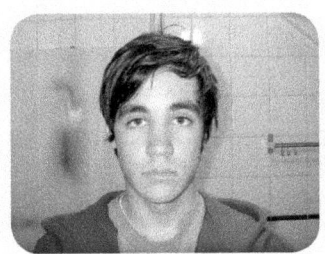

Making a LEGO minifigure walk

The fastest and easiest way to move a LEGO® minifigure is to jump forward one row at a time. However, the result looks more like a glide than a walk, more suitable for a robot. Depending on the walking pace, press 2, 3 or 4 to take multiple pictures in each position.

Actual step-by-step walking

You can make LEGO® minifigures actually appear to walk. It takes eight steps for a complete movement of left and right legs:

❶ Start with the LEGO® figure standing still with both legs straight

❷ Push the figure away from you and swing the closest leg forward. Stand the figure up again with the closest leg angled forward

❸ Rock the figure forward so that it is between rows on the base board – standing on the heel of the front foot, and toe of the back foot. Straighten its back so that the figure is standing tall

❹ Rock the figure forward again so that its closest leg is firmly connected to the next row on the base board. The back leg is angled back

❺ Pull the figure towards you and swing the back leg forward so that it is standing upright again – ONE step completed

❻ Pull the figure towards you and swing the furthest away leg forward. Stand the figure again

❼ Rock the figure forward so that it is between rows on the base board – standing on the heel of the front foot and toe of the back foot. Straighten its back so that it is standing tall

❽ Rock the figure forward again so that the furthest away leg is firmly connected to the next row on the base board. The closest leg is angled back

❾ Push the figure away from you and swing the closest leg forward so that it is standing upright again and you're back into position **❶** – a full cycle of TWO steps completed.

LEGO minifigure walk – advanced options

- With each step you can also move the figure's arms. Swing them in time with the opposite leg
- Move the head. This action may not be rhythmic but might be related to what the figure is looking at as it walks by
- Bend the figure forward at the hips and it will look like it is running
- Do the moonwalk using these poses from the above steps (for each step press 2 for two copies of the picture):
  - pose **❽**, pose **❼**, (slide back one space), pose **❼**, pose **❻**, pose **❹**, pose **❸**, (slide back one space), pose **❸**, pose **❷** and repeat.

Using replacement figures

If you are fortunate enough to have multiple sets of the same character (any medium but particularly useful with LEGO®), it can be fast and easy to simply switch the character with a replacement in a different pose. This method can also be used to simulate talking (see *Talking LEGO heads* on page 134).

LEGO® Starter Sets are an economical way to get multiple copies of the same characters and props.

Here is an example of four replacement characters for a running sequence:

Making a character talk

The way characters talk helps show their personality:

- The simplest way is to show your character clearly on screen and allow the voice-over to imply that the words are coming from that character. Often this is all that is required or possible to create the effect

- **The best way to show which character is talking is by moving that character, and keeping all other characters relatively still.** Move just the limbs or move the whole character. Either way make sure the movements are realistic in expression and timing (remember you may be recording 12 pictures for every second of movie).

  If you want a character to raise their hands, make small movements over 3–12 pictures (up to one second in real time). If you want a character to turn around while talking, make small movements over 12–24 pictures (1–2 seconds in real time). If a character gets a fright they might make a sudden movement in one picture, but in general a lot of very quick movements may produce confusion for the audience

- In addition to animated movements, use an appropriate LEGO® face expression to convey particular mood.

- If your characters are molded with Plasticine you'll need clean hands and a blunt wooden or plastic blade to gently re-mould your character's mouth shape

- You can create open and shut jaw movements with jointed toys

- If you want to make your character talk with moving lips, you'll need to know about the standard mouth shapes (the proper name for them is 'phoneme'*). Some sounds are made with an open mouth, other sounds use closed teeth or lips. If you use the appropriate sequence of mouth shapes it will look as if your character is actually speaking

- For some styles of stop motion characters, you can simply switch replacement mouths '*Mr Potato Head®*' style (see also *Talking LEGO heads* on page 134)

- In the following example, a face without a mouth has been printed or drawn on paper. Three mouth shapes have been cut out and one at a time placed in position. Once these three pictures are recorded, the animation for this scene can be achieved quickly by copying and pasting the appropriate pictures. You can download the artwork for this example at *stop-motion-handbook.com/downloads.html*.

This type of example is also great for whiteboard illustration as only the parts that change need to be redrawn (see *Whiteboard animation* on page 147)

- In *Wallace and Gromit®* movies, Wallace opens his mouth wide to express emphasis, while Gromit uses his eyebrows to communicate his thoughts

*In the early days of Disney, Blair Preston worked out that for the purpose of animation there are 10 distinct mouth shapes. Refer to *www.garycmartin.com/mouth_shapes.html* for excellent information on using mouth shapes in animation, or search the internet for *'phoneme mouth shapes'* or *'Blair Preston'*.

- Plasticine may not hold its shape with constant adjustment. In big screen stop motion movies such as *Chicken Run* they use more robust modelling materials such as silicon rubber. They use replacement heads for each mouth shape and the chickens wear scarves to hide the join.

Talking LEGO heads

Choose at least four spare LEGO® heads and make sure they are in similar condition and the same colour. With a steady hand, use a fine-tip permanent marker to create a set of faces with the following mouth shapes:

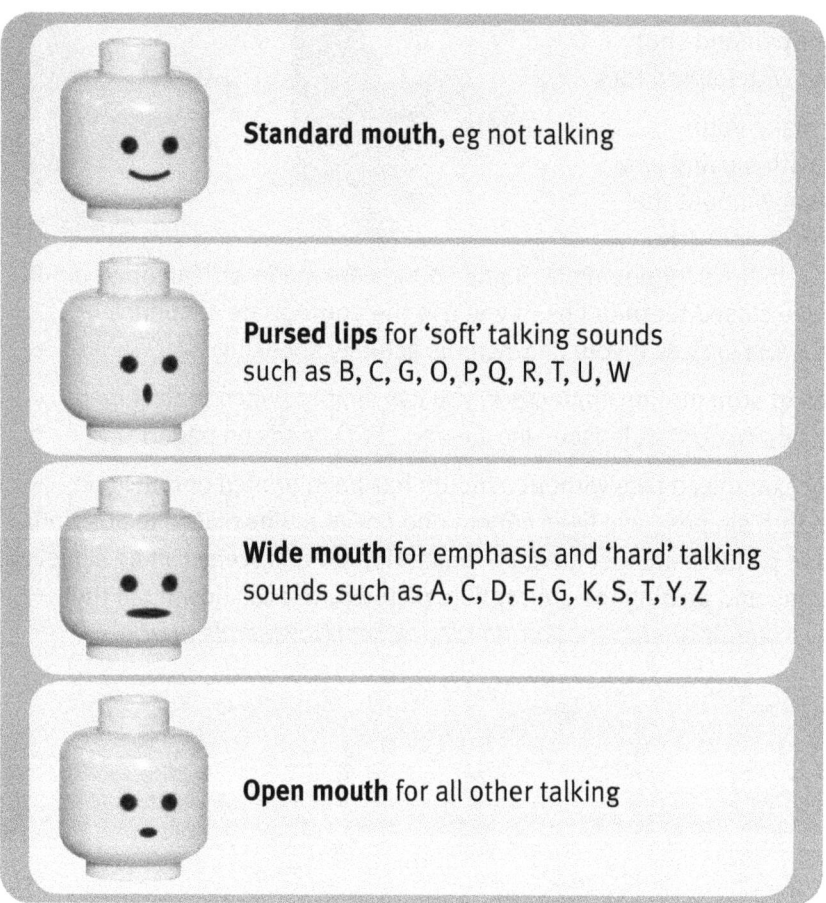

Standard mouth, eg not talking

Pursed lips for 'soft' talking sounds such as B, C, G, O, P, Q, R, T, U, W

Wide mouth for emphasis and 'hard' talking sounds such as A, C, D, E, G, K, S, T, Y, Z

Open mouth for all other talking

Putting a sentence together

One sentence at a time, write down the words to be spoken. Watch yourself in the mirror as you say the words. Pronunciation and accent can determine which mouth shape best fits with the sound.

A mouth sound is more like a syllable than a letter, so a longer word might have two or three sounds. Several words in a row might also share the same mouth shape. For example:

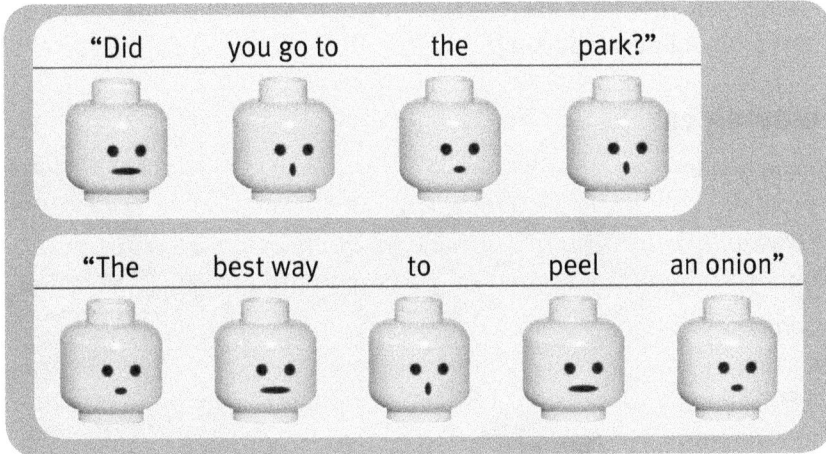

Switch replacement heads between pictures to simulate a talking mouth. Take care not to move the position of the body and keep the hat/hair back in exactly the same position. Check for any movement using the Overlay.

Refer also to iStopMotion's import video feature (see *Importing a reference video* on page 128) to import a recorded video reference of someone speaking. This helps to get the right number of mouth shapes for each word.

Making objects talk

You can bring any object to life by making it talk – fruit, toys (eg *Thomas the Tank Engine*, *Cars*), furniture etc. Create faces and/or a set of mouth shapes using drawings or cutouts from coloured card.

Creating visual effects

Big screen movies often have a wow factor because of clever camera moves and visual effects. For example, characters and objects can fly through the air and defy gravity.

There is no limit to the creativity that can be used in stop motion to achieve similar effects. Moving, flying or rotating sets or cameras usually just require sturdy platforms, tape to secure the things that shouldn't move, a rig or pivot to smoothly slide the parts that should move, and a bit of lateral thinking.

How to film a moving car

Car chases are often an action highlight in a stop motion. Here is an effective way to animate a car driving:

- Create a long narrow set, such as a street using several joining LEGO® road base plates. Add elements along both sides of the road edge such as shop fronts, sculptures, trees, traffic lights, signs, other vehicles and characters
- Position the camera looking side-on to the road at one end
- Set the camera focus on the vehicle
- For each picture, slide the road a few millimetres past the camera, use the Overlay to keep the main vehicle in the same place (in front of the camera). Animate the interactions with other vehicles and characters. Use a small piece of cotton wool to draw attention to skidding wheels.

Another interesting camera angle is to attach the camera to the vehicle giving a view from the moving vehicle.

How to fly around a set

There are many uses for an moving aerial view of the set, such as showing the vulnerability of the small character in a big set, revealing an approaching threat or just simply a beautiful pictorial segment between scenes. Big screen movies use a helicopter, crane or a drone for these moves.

In stop motion, it can be easier to rotate the set. In this example, a small LEGO® set has been built on a rotating base and has a handle out wide to manoeuvre the set. The camera view is much closer and doesn't show the edge of the set.

How to fly a rocket

Give the impression of a huge set (outer space) with this technique on a small table:

- Place a sky background on a table
- On the background place a flying craft such as a rocket or plane
- Place other items in the sky such as clouds (use cotton wool)
- Mount the camera overhead looking down on the set
- For each picture move the clouds past the craft.

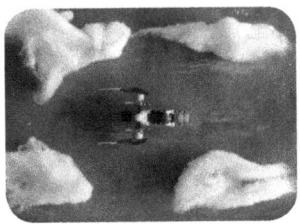  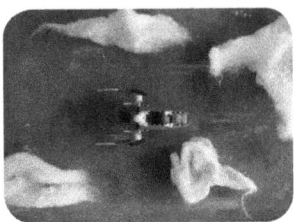

How to fire a gun

Many actions can be effectively animated if the character has realistic movements (see *Principles of animation* on page 164). Here is an example of firing a gun:

- Position the character with the gun ready to fire
- In the same picture as the shot in the soundtrack, add a coloured block on the end of the gun for the 'flash' (1 picture)
- To show the character recoil from firing – remove the flash and bend the body backwards (2-3 pictures) then gradually straighten back up again (6-12 pictures).

Don't forget, bigger guns should have a bigger flash and recoil than smaller guns.

A group of people in a parade may fire guns and recoil together, but in a battle these actions should be more random.

A machine gun effect can be achieved with a stream of alternating pictures. Record one picture with a flash and one without. Select both pictures *(they highlight blue in the Timeline)*, copy them (CMD-C) and paste (CMD-V) as many times as you need.

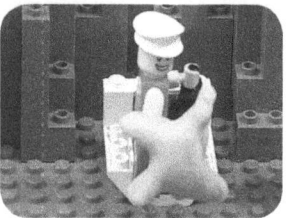 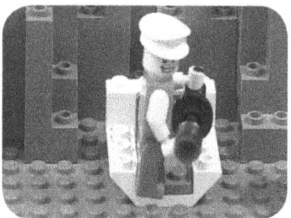 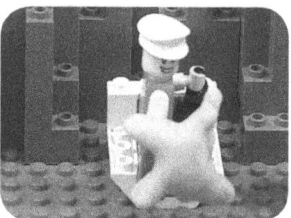

Mix Plasticine and LEGO® to create interesting gun flashes, explosions, water or blood.

Add realism and personality (even humour) to battle scenes, such as close-ups of a character turning their head to look for the target, putting the gun down to reload or taking orders on a radio.

How to make a character 'appear' out of nowhere

Because LEGO® characters easily come apart, they are suitable for portraying the effect of teleportation:

- To arrive in a scene – start with the head, then the head and body and finally the whole body (shown below)

- To exit a scene – start with the whole body, then the head and body and finally just the head.

As an alternative to creating LEGO® buildings from the ground up, it can be an interesting variation to have them appear out of the ground, roof first.

How to make things leap and jump

Add personality into your characters with life-like movements. Put a spring in their step with this tip:

- Record the pictures up to the point before the jump
- Record a second copy of the last picture before the jump
- Place the character onto a horse, skateboard, fence, bed etc. as lightly as possible, eg not pressed down, then in the next picture press the character down into the final position. Even though the figure was NOT in the air at any point, our eyes will be tricked and fill in the gaps to make us believe it was airborne.

How to make things fly

There are many ways to make things fly in a stop motion. Here are some ideas for how to achieve it:

- Use nylon string (thin, clear fishing line) to hang a plane, UFO or superhero from a sturdy overhead support eg tape a broomstick across the back of two chairs. Keep the support lower and the string shorter for a more stable the flying movement, Alternatively, mount the flying object on a thin support which can slide across the table
- Edit the pictures to remove any visible evidence of the string or support in a picture editing program (see *Editing pictures* on page 157)

- You can also convey flying by attaching the object to the camera so they move together.

  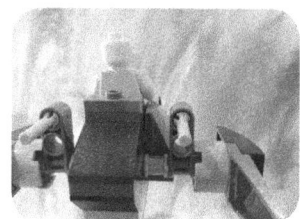

How to make a fish leap out of water

Plasticine makes really good fish because you can mould it to a realistic shape, and the shape can be changed as if the fish was swimming. It is easier to record the fish diving into the water because the fish gets smaller as it disappears below the surface:

- Make the complete fish. If you can make another one as a spare this is even better because the process requires a sharp knife to gradually slice bits off the fish
- Record the pictures which have the full fish in view
- Picture by picture as the fish dives beneath the water (table or backdrop in this case) carefully use a sharp blade to cut a slice off the fish. Use the Overlay to accurately reposition the fish with the previous picture.

When the fish comes out of the water (see below) you'll need to add Plasticine to make the fish larger. It is often easier to record this sequence backwards, then select the pictures and select Edit⟶Reverse Order.

 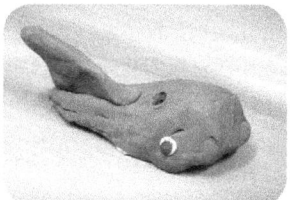 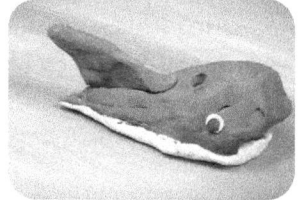

How to cut to a flashback or dream sequence

Flashbacks and dreams happen at a different time period to the main story.

A flashback will often be accompanied by a woosh sound effect and so the transition to the flashback may take 2 to 4 seconds (24 – 48 pictures). Use one of these methods to show the transition:

- Start with an empty stage, then picture by picture, piece by piece, build the set and have characters slide into position in a robotic way
- From the current scene in the main story, tilt the camera upwards to show just background sky as you blur the manual focus
- Slide a colourful object past the front of the lens at a distance where it is out of focus. When the object completely obscures the camera view, change the set. Then continue to slide the object past the lens until the new set is revealed.

Once in the actual flashback or dream, adjust the colour scheme (see *Colour correction* on page 116) or change the lighting to distinguish it from the main story. Alternatively, leave the colour correction unchanged and afterwards export the relevant frames. Adjust the colour correction and when you reimport the frames to iStopMotion the colour of those frames will be adjusted.

Both the transition effect and colour change are editing effects that can also be done in iMovie (see *Adding transitions* on page 177 and *Adjusting the clip* on page 178).

How to create lightning

In the real world lighting is seen before it is heard. In stop motion try matching the sound and change to set lighting to create a powerful effect:

- In the same picture as the lightning starts in the soundtrack shine a bright light on the set to washout the colours and detail (1 picture)
- Hold a large piece of card above the set to block room light and darken the colours and detail (1 picture)
- Shine a light from higher above the set to slightly washout the picture (1 picture)
- Hold a large piece of card higher above the set to slightly darken it (1 picture).

How to create an electric title

Animated text can easily be achieved with stop motion. Here is a method that could be used for a title or scene name:

- Create or draw the title on whiteboard or paper and record a picture
- Use the Overlay to recreate or redraw the title in the same general position but formed slightly differently and record a picture

- Select both frames and copy (CMD-C)
- Paste (CMD-V) 12 times to give 24 pictures (two seconds of animation, at 12 FPS).

How to record a scene transition

The most common transition in big screen movies is a straight cut (no transition) or a short cross dissolve. Some transitions can be added later in iMovie, as long as you've recorded additional pictures at the start and end of each scene. Transition effects can also be achieved directly in stop motion if you can create the effect live on the stage. Here is one method:

- Prepare the camera position before the transition so that the focus is set to a point in the middle of the stage. Record the scene
- Slide a colourful and translucent object (such as a stack of coloured plastic drinking cups) directly in front of the camera so they appear blurry and out of focus. The number of pictures for the movement will depend on the required duration of the transition
- When the scene is obscured with the cups, change the scene
- Then continue to slide the cups past the camera to reveal the new scene.

Transitions can be achieved on set with other materials such as cotton wool.

How to dramatise an action sequence

Engage your audience in an action sequence by moving the camera as if it is one of the characters (see *Rule 2* on page 122). This technique can be used for any situation where the characters interact physically such as in a battle, sports or a dance.

The picture below shows the set up for an action scene (this is an example of the wide stage described on page 81). Here is an example of how to record an action sequence between two characters (picture rate 12 FPS):

A stop motion stage, with a wide curved background, ready to record an action sequence

- **Wide view** (12 to 24 pictures)
  Start with an overall shot of the scene so that we see all the characters involved. This may already be achieved in the preceding pictures

- **Close-up of first character** (6 pictures)
  Move the camera onto the stage to the viewpoint of the second character (the one who receives the first blow) and reset manual focus. The goal is to have the first character approach the point of impact. Picture by picture, either move the character closer to the camera, or move the camera closer to the character

- **Impact** (1 picture)
  There are many ways to achieve an impact, such as: a) an out of focus extreme close-up of the chest of the first character, b) a white object placed in front of the scene to almost block out the camera view.

c) Batman style – write the word 'POW' or 'WHACK' with a marker on a sheet of coloured paper. Copy this picture (CMD-C) and paste it 5 times (CMD-V)

- **Recoil of second character** (12 to 24 pictures)
  Move the camera to the viewpoint of the first character or a side-on view of character Two and reset focus. The second character should be either flying backwards through the air or skidding along the ground, as if out of control

- **Response of second character** (12 to 24 pictures)
  Move the camera to a close-up of the second character as they pick themselves up and return to deliver a counter blow. Reset focus. This could be broken into several parts – an extreme close-up of their face, and then their whole body as they stand up to face their opponent

- **Regroup** (12 to 24 pictures)
  Move the camera to another view of the whole scene, and reset focus.

Timing

Timing is a very important aspect for creating convincing actions. Among other things, timing shows the emotion of the character. A quick response in a battle shows energy so actions usually take less than a second (less than 12 pictures). A slow action could indicate just slowness, or when combined with head movements (eg looking to camera) could show cunning and courage. Slow actions usually take 4 seconds or longer (requiring at least 48 pictures). Impact and gunshot actions are instant and may take just one picture.

Vary the length of picture sequences to match the actions in the story. A steady stream of camera movements with less than 12 pictures will seem like a visual assault to the audience. Adding longer sequences allows anticipation and emphasis so that faster actions have more effect (see *Principles of animation* on page 164).

Simulate actions

Decide how your character should move by simulating the action yourself or asking someone to demonstrate. Notice whether the whole body moves or just the head or arms (see also *Importing a reference video* on page 128).

Add more realism by making objects 'bounce' after a sudden movement, eg if someone falls over. Once they hit the floor, record another picture with them slightly raised before they finally rest on the ground (see *Principles of animation* on page 164).

How to create an epic stop motion movie

As a general rule we suggest keeping the number of characters and elements in a scene to a small manageable number. Three characters per scene is often enough to carry the story – a lead character, someone for them to relate to and an extra character. This limited cast also leads to quick and efficient animation.

However, within most movie makers there lingers a desire to create something epic.

EPIC: an ambitious style of film-making with large scale, sweeping scope and spectacle, often transporting the audience to other settings.

To create an epic feel in your stop motion find one scene where you can use a big set, or have a large number of characters on the set. It will be more effective if this scene has dramatic music.

Illustration animation

You can record a stop motion creating a painting or illustration by recording a picture after each pen or brush stroke.

Tips

- Position the camera directly facing the artwork – not slanted or at an angle. If your work is on a table, mount the camera overhead (see *Flat 2D animation* on page 148). If you use an easel, mount the camera so the lens is parallel to the artwork
- Firmly secure the camera tripod and work surface so they can't move
- Arrange lights from above the canvas so that your body won't cast a shadow
- Use diffusers or bounce boards to get an even brightness across the canvas (see *Lighting* on page 100)
- Set the camera's white balance and exposure
- Make sure the camera view is smaller than the canvas or paper so you don't see the edge of the sheet
- Turn on the Action Safe guide to assist keeping important details away from the edge of the screen. In the example shown, the feet are too close to the bottom.

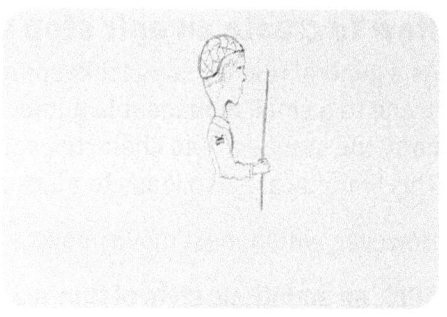

For other examples search *'stop motion painting'* on YouTube, or go to *http://blublu.org*

Whiteboard animation

Another very flexible medium for stop motion is a whiteboard. It is easy to draw pictures, erase parts and redraw them to get real animation.

Tips

In addition to all the tips on the previous page, here are tips for successful whiteboard stop motion:

- Whiteboards are highly reflective. Position the camera and whiteboard to avoid glare or reflection and put a shade or diffuser over lights
- Wear white clothes to limit reflection
- Clean the whiteboard thoroughly before you start
- Use new whiteboard markers
- Use a cloth to cleanly erase unwanted details. Shadows from previous drawings can ruin the animation and make it look sloppy
- Lay a printed page on the flat surface to set the manual focus
- Set the camera's white balance and exposure, then leave the camera and mount alone. Don't bump the camera
- Add interest by including sequences showing the artist's hand on the artwork as if they were stretching or moving things with their fingers.

For other examples search *'whiteboard stop motion'*, or *'minilogue/hitchhikers choice'* on YouTube, or go to www.thersa.org/discover/videos/rsa-animate

To create more professional results of whiteboard animation (not strictly stop motion) try these options:

- **Videoscribe** (*www.videoscribe.co*)
- **Explaindio Video Creator** (*http://explaindio.com/2/jvzoo*) creates a wide range of video effects including whiteboard type animation which they call doodle sketches and an amazing feature called sketch to video which creates actual video as a whiteboard animation

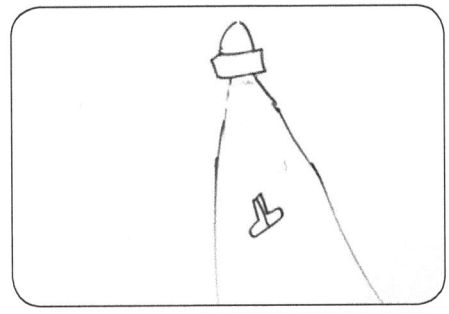

Flat 2D animation

There are many art forms which are best recorded on a flat table surface, such as:

- Coloured paper cutouts
- Flat Plasticine sculptures
- Whiteboard
- Any medium where gravity would make it difficult to stay vertical.

Tips

- Mount the camera directly overhead looking downward. If your tripod doesn't allow this, make a vertical mount out of wood (see *How to make a camera mount* on page 98). In either case, make sure the camera has a counterbalance weight to stop it tipping over and damaging the camera or yourself
- Position the tripod at the top of the working space to keep it out of your way. In iStopMotion, set Orientation on the Recording pane to 'Rotate 180°' to keep the camera view the right way around
- Position lights to avoid shadows of the camera, tripod or people
- Check for glare and reflections from windows or room lights
- Lay a printed page on the flat surface to set the manual focus
- Set the camera's white balance and exposure, then leave the camera and mount alone. Don't bump it!

Hang a counterbalance weight here

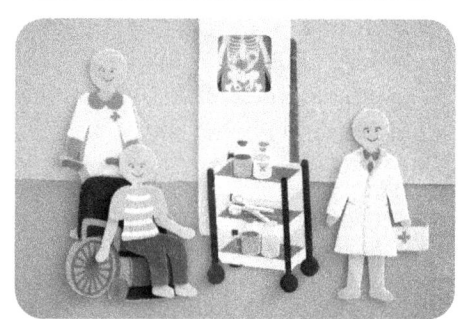

Two level stop motion

Take a series of still photos of an activity such as a person walking.

Develop these as prints and write the sequence number on the back of each one (it is vital they don't get out of order).

Place these photos one at a time on top of each other putting the action in the photos into a new context, eg swinging on bars in a playground becomes swinging up an electrical cable.

Tips

- Keep the person in the centre of each still photo
- Match the movements in the still photos with the planned stop motion actions, eg jumping, climbing

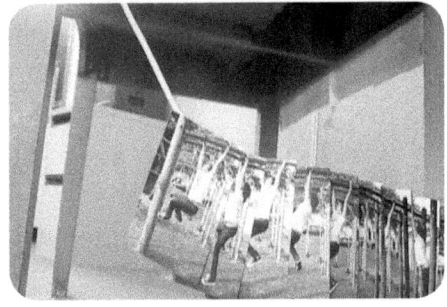

- Portrait-shape (tall) photos will produce an effect where multiple people are seen (see top examples)
- Landscape shape (wide) photos should cover the person in the photo underneath (see example with mouse)

- Set the iStopMotion Frame Rate at 2 pictures per second
- Keep the tripod steady and animate the photos across the screen, or move the camera as you lay each photo. Use iStopMotion's Overlay feature to keep the person's torso in same position.

See this example at *www.acumen.net.nz/pages/NMSClassPhoto.html* For other examples search *'the PEN story'* on YouTube.

Time lapse – security system

Use the time lapse features in iStopMotion to build your own security system. Set a camera in a hidden place and start iStopMotion recording.

This could be a fun thing to do at home while you are out for the day. When you come home you'll be able to see who has been in the room.

Calculate the capture rate

As a reliable security system, you need to record enough pictures to trace movements, but not too many that it is too long to watch. Refer to page 112 for Time lapse calculations.

Tips

- Make sure expensive equipment is secure
- A wide angle perspective of a whole room is one type of project where your computer's iSight camera could be suitable
- To add the actual time, make sure the camera can see a wall clock.

When using Time Lapse as a security system:

- Select iStopMotion menu ⇢Preferences, and on the General panel and turn off the option 'Beep during Time Lapse'
- Hide the iStopMotion document window by clicking on the yellow 'Hide' button in the top left of the window.

Tilt shift - miniatures

Turn a drab panorama into a real life miniature. This stylised effect is called Tilt Shift, which sets part of the screen to be in focus and the rest to fade into a blur.

- On the Recording pane move the slider to turn on Tilt Shift. Click the Configure button to display a line with two dots

- Drag each end of the line to show the plane that should be in focus

- Click either of the dots and drag away from the line to indicate how much of the picture is to be in focus

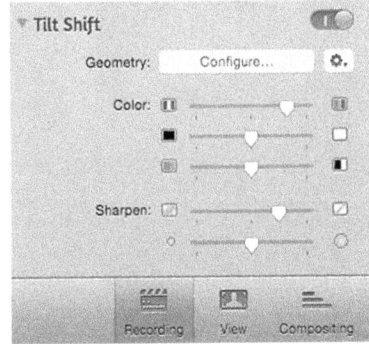

- Adjust the sliders to set the colour (saturation, brightness and contrast) and sharpen (sharpen and intensify). These sliders introduce the 'toy like' appearance. The Colour sliders for Tilt Shift create surreal colour schemes that are much brighter than in real life

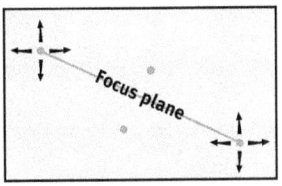 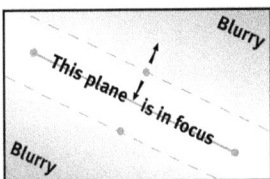

- This effect can be used with regular stop motion and is very effective with time lapse.

To apply Tilt Shift to an existing stop motion

If after recording a stop motion you wish you had used Tilt Shift, you can:

- Select all frames in the movie (CMD-A)
- Select File⟶Export Selection⟶As Images
- Open a new movie (File⟶New)
- Set the required Tilt Shift setting
- Select Movie⟶Import Images⟶from Disk...

For other examples search *'stop motion tilt shift'* on YouTube.

Common stop motion mistakes

One of the best ways to learn is to watch stop motions other people have made. Many common beginner mistakes are relatively easy to overcome with practice.

Some pictures not in focus – set camera to manual focus. Auto focus generally makes the centre of the screen sharp and in focus. So when a character moves away from the centre the camera tries to focus on the new thing in the centre and the character may become blurry

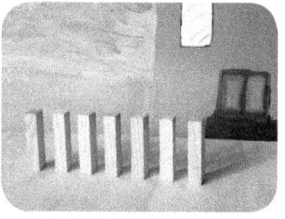 

Bumped camera position – secure the camera on a sturdy mount, or move the camera to a completely new position to disguise the bump

Hand in shot – wait until everyone is clear before taking a picture

 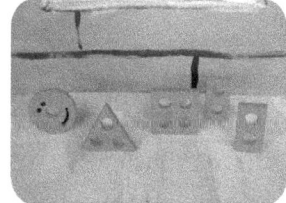

Variable lighting – use artificial light for more constant lighting. Lock the camera's white balance and exposure to reduce random changes

Uneven lighting – change the lighting set up. Add more light on dark parts and reduce light on bright parts. Use a diffuser to soften the light

Shadows – (unless you want this effect deliberately) – add another light from a different angle or use a diffuser to soften the light

Background shadows – make sure everyone stands clear of the stage and lighting, or stands in exactly the same spot during every picture

Too dark – use more lights or adjust the camera settings

Camera angle – engage the audience in the story by placing the camera at the character's eye level

Camera not level – make sure the camera is level with the set, unless angles are part of the story

Poor framing – take time setting up each scene. Position the camera to clearly show the characters. Make sure all detail is within the Action Safe area and use the 'Rule of Thirds'

Edge of stage visible – move the camera or background

Reflections – some surfaces, such as whiteboards, are prone to reflections. Rotate the whiteboard to a different angle or put a diffuser over the light

Reflections on character faces – make sure your set is not in direct line of window glare across the room. Use sheets of card around the set to block reflections

Visible dirt, particularly in close-ups – use a cloth and small brush to clean and dust your sets and characters. Make sure you have clean hands, particularly when handling Plasticine characters

Scrabble
by PES

Commercial for Scrabble's 60th Anniversary. *www.youtube.com/watch?v=P_HW5oGsLlw* Go to *www.pesfilm.com* for more examples by PES.

Advanced iStopMotion

Compositing pane

The Compositing pane lets you combine stop motion pictures with other images. Click the Compositing button on the Toolbar (CMD-3).

Adding a foreground

If you want to put something in front of your pictures such as a window frame, add a foreground graphic.

- Select one of the images provided or click the Source button and navigate to the folder containing the image you want to use

- The foreground image must be the same shape as your stop motion (eg HD 720 is 1280 x 720 pixels, DV PAL Widescreen is 720 x 576 pixels) or it will be distorted. Go to iStopMotion menu⋯⋯⋗Preferences and check Movie Presets panel for information about the size of your movie. If the image is not the same shape, open it in an image editing program and crop it to the same shape as the movie

- Foreground images need to have transparency information (called an alpha channel) to let the camera picture show through. You can use PNG and TIFF file formats

- The foreground image can be changed and is not added to the pictures until the movie is exported

- You can only have one foreground per iStopMotion movie. If you want to use more foregrounds, break your movie into several short stop motion clips and join them together in iMovie (see *Editing stop motion clip to make a movie* on page 171).

Adding a background

Adding a picture in the background is iStopMotion's version of 'green screen'. Set up your stage with any solid colour background (see *Green screen stage* on page 82). iStopMotion will replace the solid colour with the background image. Now your stop motion can really take place under water or on the moon. Consider the following tips:

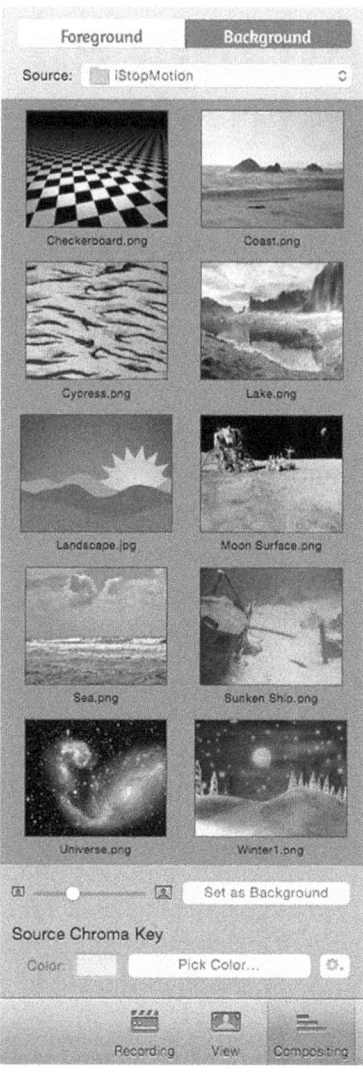

- The background colour on the stage can be any solid colour, but must be different to the colours in your characters or props
- Some paint shops and art supply shops sell Chroma Blue and Chroma Green paint. Use it to paint props or supports that you want to 'disappear'
- The background image must be the same shape as your stop motion or it will be distorted (see note under *Adding a foreground* on page 155)
- Background images need to be in one of these popular file formats: PNG, PSD, JPG and TIFF
- Keep the camera in the same position (no panning, zooming or moving), because the background photo doesn't move
- You can only use one background per iStopMotion movie. If you want to use more backgrounds, break your movie into several short clips and join them together in iMovie (see *Editing stop motion clip to make a movie* on page 171)
- The key to the 'green screen' effect is having bright and even lighting on the background (see *Lighting* on page 100).

Editing pictures

The ideal way to record a stop motion is to create the set for each scene and record the pictures. However, as you get more adventurous, you may want to edit some pictures to create an effect that could not be achieved in the set. For example:

Fix a mistake – remove a visible blob of Blu-Tack

Hide a support – to remove the rod used to suspend an aerial action

Enhance a scene – change an expression on a character's face

Add special effects – add flashes of light to simulate gunfire

Add invisible details – add sky writing

Editing one picture at a time

You can edit pictures one at a time directly from iStopMotion if you have specified an image editor (iStopMotion menu⟶Preferences ⟶Helpers) such as Adobe Photoshop or Acorn (*www.flyingmeat.com/acorn*):

- Right-click the thumbnail in the Timeline and select 'Edit in (image editor)' and it will automatically open in the image editor
- Make the required changes to the picture
- Close the image and Save it. The edited image is automatically updated in iStopMotion.

Editing a series of pictures

- Select the pictures you want to edit (click the thumbnail of the first picture you want to edit, hold Shift and click the last thumbnail. If you want to edit all pictures, press CMD-A)
- Select File⟶Export Selection⟶ As Images. A copy of each picture is saved to the folder you specify, with file names 'stop motion name_picture number.png', eg 'moon landing_15.png'. It may be easier to create a new folder for these images
- From the desktop, open the pictures in an image editing program such as Adobe Photoshop, or Acorn
- Make the required changes
- Save the files
- In iStopMotion, make sure the playhead is at the picture immediately before the first edited picture
- Select Movie⟶Import Images⟶From Disk
- Shift-click to select the series of edited pictures you want to import
- Click Import
- Delete the original unedited pictures from the Timeline if you haven't already.

Stop motion with a digital still camera

Another good method for stop motion involves taking pictures on a digital still camera, phone or MP3 player. It doesn't matter what device you use as long as the pictures can be uploaded to a computer. You are not tied to a computer so you can go anywhere, for example:

- bus trip – looking out the window
- following someone walking – forwards or backwards
- house being built
- street parade (in it or watching it).

These types of stop motion don't need a traditional script, but planning and coordinating a logical sequence of movements will result in a better stop motion than a sequence of random shots. Planning will also make sure you record the right number of pictures.

In the following example, a group of children are sitting on the ground. The camera is on a tripod and has a remote shutter release to avoid touching the camera. In each photo the children move forward, so the stop motion will look like they are driving imaginary cars and crashing.

Step 1: Planing your animation

The general options for recording movement are:

- **Move only the object.** Put your camera on a tripod and use a remote shutter release to avoid touching the camera. Move only the object and take care not to move the background or camera

- **Move both the camera AND the object** so it appears you are travelling with the object. Regardless of how the object moves, the camera needs to make an identical movement so that the object stays in the same position in each picture. Without the iStopMotion Overlay feature, you are relying on other means of ensuring accuracy and consistency between pictures. Create a composition guide on your viewfinder with an outline drawn on an overlay of plastic, or markings on Post-it® notes (see picture). Put the camera on a tripod or mount and use a tape measure to retain a constant distance between the camera and the 'object'

- **Move the camera only.** You'll get the best results if the camera is on a tripod, although with a handheld camera you may produce an acceptable result. Try moving the camera around a stationary elevated object for an impressive effect like *The Matrix* where the object seems frozen in space (to remove supports and threads, see *Editing pictures* on page 157).

Step 2: Recording the pictures

If you are using a multi mega-pixel still camera, reduce the size of the pictures to one of the smaller settings because this will be closer to the size required for the stop motion picture size (see *Picture size* on page 108). It also speeds up the process to import the pictures. For example, a stop motion using HD720 requires pictures that are 1280 x 720 pixels.

Taking pictures of people has particular challenges because people move parts of their body you don't want moving. And you don't have the Overlay feature to show what has moved and what hasn't. As well as the general instruction of having people move in a particular direction, eg take a step backwards and take time to check that someone hasn't randomly changed their posture, arm position or head direction:

- Set up the camera on a mount or tripod and arrange the picture composition. It may be useful to add markers such as tape on the floor

- Ask each person to take note of their starting posture (arms, legs, head position) and remind them either to keep this constant, or if there is an action, such as pointing or waving, to make very small movements between pictures (remember 12 pictures will play back in only one second, although this type of stop motion may be suitable for 6 FPS)

- Agree with everyone the distance you want them to move between each picture, eg shuffle forward one step, and practise this movement.

Taking the pictures:
- Have everyone move into position
- Check that the person, or object, is aligned with your camera viewfinder
- Call "ready" two seconds before you take the picture to give everyone the chance to get into 'posture' position
- Take the picture
- Give instruction about how people should move, eg slide left leg forward 10 cm
- Repeat these steps.

If you make a mistake, or take a picture before everyone was ready, you may be tempted to immediately delete that picture on the camera, but **don't.** You risk moving the camera and ruining the alignment of all your pictures. Just take another shot and delete the wrong one later.

Step 3: Uploading the pictures

Now that you've taken the pictures, you need to get them onto the computer and into iStopMotion.

If the pictures are still on the camera:
- Connect the camera to the computer
- Open a new iStopMotion file and select the Preset image size
- Select Movie⟶Import Images⟶from Still Camera
- Select the pictures you want to import. If you want all the pictures on the camera press CMD-A
- Click Import
- Select File⟶Save to save your stop motion.

If the pictures are in a folder on the computer:
Use this method if you can connect your camera to your computer, but the camera is not compatible with iStopMotion:
- Connect the camera to the computer and transfer the photos to a folder
- *(Optional)* Select the images and double-click – they will open in the application Preview. Delete the wrong shots. This can also be done later in iStopMotion
- Open a new iStopMotion file and select the Preset image size
- Select Movie⟶Import Images⟶from Disk

- Select the folder of pictures you want to import. If you want all the pictures in the folder press CMD-A
- Click Import
- Select File⟶Save to save your stop motion.

If the pictures are in iPhoto

iPhoto can create slideshows, but is not designed for rapid display of pictures.
You need to get a copy of the pictures out of iPhoto and into iStopMotion:

- Open iPhoto
- Select the pictures you want (it may be easier to create an album in iPhoto to group the pictures)
- Drag the pictures to an empty folder on the desktop (you can delete this folder when you have made your stop motion as the originals are still in iPhoto)
- Open a new iStopMotion file and select the Preset image size
- In iStopMotion select Movie⟶Import Images⟶from Disk
- Select the folder of pictures you want to import. If you want all the pictures in the folder press CMD-A
- Click Import
- Select File⟶Save to save your stop motion.

Step 4: Editing in iStopMotion

Take time to check that the photos are suitable for the animation effect:

- Press CMD-Home to show the first thumbnail in the Timeline
- Press OPT-1 to show only the pictures without any overlay of the camera view
- Press the right arrow to click through each picture fixing any problems such as:
  - duplicate pictures *(delete extra pictures)*
  - mistake pictures *(delete bad pictures)*
  - pictures out of order *(drag thumbnails into the correct order)*
  - wrong animation speed *(create a new iStopMotion file with a different picture rate (FPS) and reimport all pictures)*
  - wrong animation speed in some places *(add or delete pictures to correct the action speed).*

When each you've confirmed each picture is correct watch your movie at proper speed:

- Press CMD-Home to show the first thumbnail in the Timeline
- Press P to play.

Planning a complex stop motion

Some stop motion projects involve the movement of many elements and the only way to successfully achieve these is with planning:

- Plan your animation on a computer first. This is to test your idea, show your helpers what you want to achieve, and give you a specific plan to be efficient on the recording day
- Have realistic expectations – each picture could take several minutes to set up
- Use templates and guides to assist making the movements accurately
- Participants may have limited attention spans and need breaks.

'Deadline Post it stop motion'
Search YouTube for *'Post it stop motion'* by Bang-Yao Liu (*www.youtube.com/watch?v=BpWMoFNPZSs*)

'Last leaf' music video
www.okgo.net/category/videos

'Pac man'
People stop motion by Guillaume Reymond *www.notsonoisy.com*.
There are many other stop motion examples on this website.

'Parkour'
Search YouTube for *'Stop-Motion Parkour'* by CorridorDigital (*www.youtube.com/watch?v=g3p2TZ5q9to*)

'Moving on'
Go to *www.aardman.com* and search for *'Moving On'*.
There are many other stop motion examples on this website.

Principles of animation

These principles, developed by Disney animators in the early 1930s, help to create believable characters. The animators figured out how to make things look alive, and make characters look like they are thinking and reacting rather than just moving around like robots.

1) Squash and stretch

Squashing and stretching exaggerates object deformations. For example, when a ball bounces on the floor, it squashes flat.

When an object squashes and stretches, it must maintain the same mass, but just changes shape. Plasticine squashes really well; LEGO® does not.

2) Anticipation

Anticipation guides the audience's eyes to where the action is about to occur. One of the biggest problems in beginners' movies is that it can be hard to tell what's going on because characters do things suddenly for no apparent reason. For example, if a character is walking and suddenly something is in their hands, the viewer will probably be surprised because there was no indication of the impending action.

Draw attention to the action that's about to happen through anticipation. Have the character look at the thing, and then bend to pick it up.

3) Follow-through

Follow-through occurs after an action. For example, after throwing a ball, the character's hand won't just stop, it will continue moving as it returns back to a normal position.

Follow-through actions include the reactions of the character after an action, eg leap for joy, shrug of shoulders, and usually lets the audience know how the character feels about what has just happened.

4) Arcs

Everything in nature tends to move in arcs or curves rather than perfectly straight lines. Using arcs to animate the movements of characters helps achieve a natural look. Movements in straight lines make a character appear robotic or sinister.

Gravity also makes things move in arcs. If you throw something, it will curve up toward its high point and then curve down towards the ground.

5) Slow-in and slow-out

Most things have a tendency to start and stop moving gradually.

For example, if a character is going to run, they won't start at full speed and then stop instantly. They should build up speed gradually and then slow down gradually.

6) Timing

Timing adds emotion and intention to a character's actions. both in:

- Physical timing: the actual motions and time required to perform an action
- Theatrical timing: the pauses and emphases that make an action dramatic.

7) Secondary action

Secondary actions are little movements that aren't essential but help to add meaning to an action.

For example, if a character licks his lips as he picks up an apple it shows he expects the apple to be juicy and is anticipating the taste.

8) Exaggeration

Exaggeration is a good way to add emphasis to certain movements and draw attention where you want it. A lot of exaggeration can be achieved with *Squash and stretch*.

If your movie is about something realistic, keep exaggeration to a minimum, but if it is a comedy – use exaggeration liberally.

An action can be further exaggerated with accompanying sound effects.

9) Staging

Staging is the art of using camera angle, camera movement, lighting, composition, placement of characters and props to direct the viewer's eye. Staging means composing your shots so that the action is clear and the viewer can easily tell what's going on.

10) Solid modelling

Animated shapes need to have a clear shape and solid appearance to come to life. Solid modelling helps to convey the weight, depth and balance of the character. Plasticine and LEGO® have a solid appearance and work well for stop motion. Other mediums such as whiteboard can have characters with solid shapes, whereas stick figures appear flimsy.

11) Appeal

Character personality or appeal helps the emotional connection between character and audience. Characters must be well developed, have an interesting personality, and a clear set of desires or needs that drive their behaviour and actions.

An audience wants to know that they can relate to characters in a story and that it is worth their time watching the movie.

Lastly, no one wants a bad movie review. Emphasising these tips will help you to avoid one!

Adapted from *http://en.wikipedia.org/wiki/12_basic_principles_of_animation* and *www.stopmotionanimation.com*

Edit and publish

In many cases your stop motion was completed in iStopMotion once you've taken the last picture. Well done!

At other times, you may need to edit your stop motion – combine it with another stop motion or real video clips, add a title and credits, add transitions between scenes or adjust the overall colouring.

In this chapter you will use iMovie to edit the stop motion, and publish it as a movie. You will learn about:

- Editing in iMovie
- Saving your movie.

iMovie

These notes are only an introduction to iMovie. They relate to typical editing that may be required to complete a stop motion. For more information about the wider features of iMovie go to *www.apple.com/findouthow/movies*.

The iMovie window

❶ Libraries
The Libraries sidebar has two parts. At the top are lists of events, projects and imported media such as video, audio and images. At the bottom are lists of editing content – Transitions, Titles, Maps, Backgrounds, music and sounds from iTunes.

You can show or hide the sidebar with the Libraries button to create more space for the Timeline.

❷ Browser
View and select clips from the selected Library ❶.

❸ Viewer
Play video clips from the Browser ❷ or Timeline ❹.

❹ Timeline
Assemble, arrange and edit clips to create the movie.

170

Editing stop motion clip to make a movie

We'll use iMovie for adding the title and credits to the stop motion. In many cases this might be all that is needed to complete the movie.

Then we'll look at some of the other editing features which may be useful for a bigger stop motion movie project.

Creating an iMovie project

To create a new movie project:

- Click the New button ➕ in the top left. If you don't see this button, click the Projects button in the top left or press CMD-N
- Click Movie

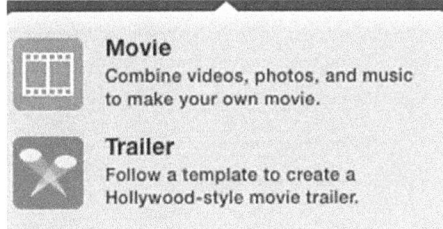

- Select 'No Theme' until you are certain which one you want. Themes add high quality titles and transitions to movies. They can also be applied later
- Click Create
- Name your movie and select the Event folder or this movie.

All iMovie projects are saved in folders called **Events,** usually grouped by recording date or occasion. This makes it easy to keep related clips together and to find your movies in future.

To import the stop motion clip (created in iStopMotion):

- Click the Import button ⬇
- Make sure the appropriate Event is listed at the top of the window
- Select the stop motion (possibly saved in the Movies folder)
- Click Import Selected – *the clip appears in the Browser* ❷.

Adding clips to the Timeline

Now that the stop motion clip is in iMovie the movie can be created in the Timeline:

- Click the My Media button at the top of the Browser ❷ to view the clips
- Select the appropriate Event in the Libraries List ❶. The clips for imported for this project may appear under Project Media at the top of the list
- Double-click clip in the Browser ❷ to select the entire clip. If you only want part of the clip click and drag over the portion you want
- If you need to see more in the Browser click the Thumbnail button ☼ at the top and adjust the zoom and size of the clips
- Click the Add Selection button + to add the clip to the Timeline ❹.

You can also drag clips and other media directly from the desktop into the Browser, or into the Timeline. The Timeline shows a representative strip of the pictures.

The audio waveform can appear under the pictures. To show or hide the audio waveforms click the Settings button in the top right of the Timeline.

Fade in from black at the start and F*ade out to black* at the end are useful effects.

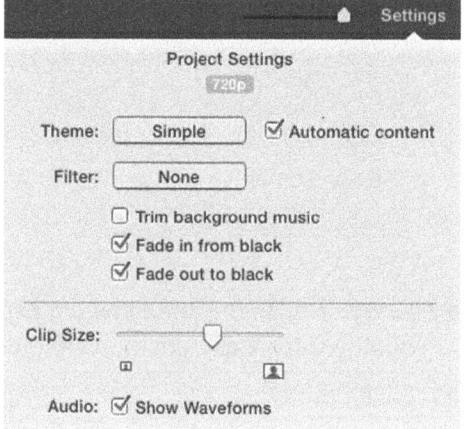

Adding titles

The most common editing task for simple stop motion movies may be to add titles. In this book we've outlined the steps to prepare your stop motion for titles by allowing space in the soundtrack (see *Audio for title and credits* on page 46) and in the pictures for the title and credits (see *Title* on page 121 and *Credits* on page 123). If you need other text in your movies, eg scene names, subtitles, explanatory notes etc, use a title.

Some title styles are simple, while others are quite sophisticated and animated. If you have selected a theme for the movie you can also choose additional theme title styles.

Click the Titles button at the top of the Browser ❷.

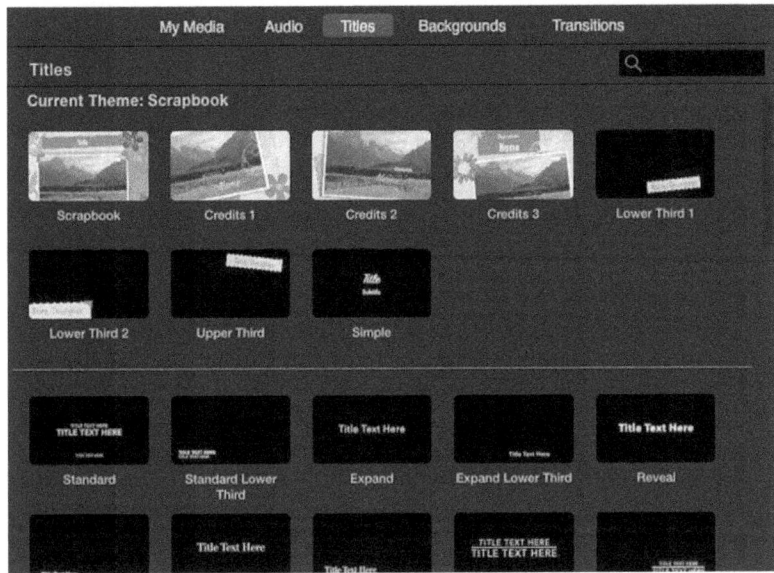

Move the cursor over the title styles in the Browser ❷ to see its animation effect. Scroll the Browser window to see all the styles.

When you have chosen the title style you want to use, drag it into the Timeline ❹ – *a purple bar appears above the clip:*

- Drag a title style **onto the start** of the clip and it will be added for 8 seconds
- Drag a credits style **onto the end** of the clip and it will be added for 8 seconds
- Drag the title style **above** the clip and it will be added for 4 seconds at the Playhead. Some styles such as 'Scrolling Credits' are longer
- Drag a title style **before or after** the clip and it will be added with a black background.

Enter your words into the title and then we'll adjust the timing:

- To **enter your text**, double-click on the purple title bar, click into the text field in the Viewer ❸ and type your text
- To **change the font**, double-click on the purple title bar, then click the text in the Viewer ❸. Select a font from the list of iMovie fonts, or to choose another font from your computer select 'Show Fonts…' from the bottom of the list. You can also change the size and colour of the text and apply bold, italic or outline styles.

To adjust the timing of the title (use the Timeline Zoom slider for a larger, more accurate, view) .

As you make adjustments to the position of a title watch the Viewer ❸:

173

- To **move** a title to show at a different time, drag the centre of the purple bar to a new position along the Timeline
- To adjust the **length** of the title, drag either end of the purple bar to shorten or lengthen it. Titles need to display for at least two seconds so they can be read. Scrolling credits may need more than 10 seconds to scroll at the right speed. Titles look better if they also fit at the start or end with a change in the picture or a beat in the music.

If there is not enough space at the end of the stop motion for the credits, add a background (see *Adding backgrounds* on page 176), or add a photo (see *Adding images* on page 176), and maybe add a transition between them (see *Adding transitions* on page 177).

Play the movie

To play the movie in iMovie at a larger size than the Viewer, click the Full Screen button . Press ESC to cancel.

> If your movie is now complete, go to *Saving the movie* on page 180.

Adding other movie elements

Adding music or sound effects (if required)

Music and sound effects added in iMovie are additional to any soundtrack already in the stop motion. It is often easier to create the complete soundtrack in GarageBand before recording the stop motion pictures. But if music or sound effects need to be added in iMovie, here is an overview:

- Click the Audio button at the top of the Browser ❷

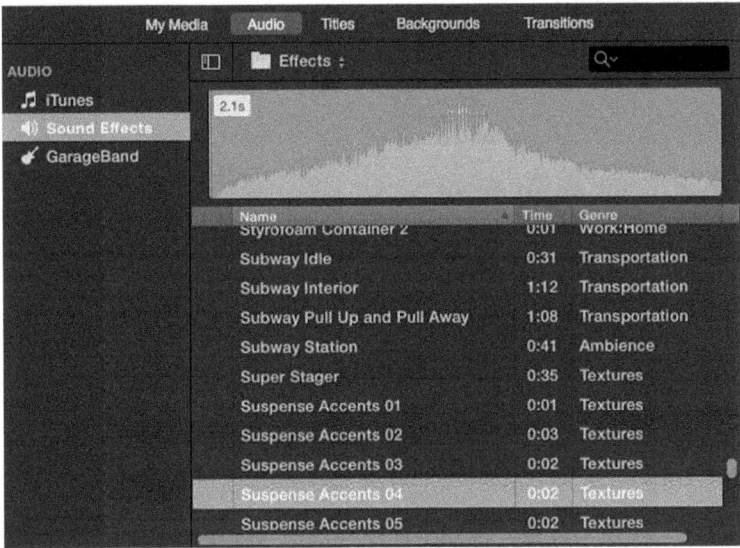

- Click on the Play button in the left column to listen to the music or sound effect
- Drag the name of the sound to the position in the Timeline ❹ where you want it – *a green bar appears under the clip.*

    You can also drag audio files directly from the desktop into the Timeline ❹.
    You can add several sounds to play at the same time.

To adjust the sound (use the Timeline Zoom slider for a larger, more accurate, view):

- To **move** audio to play at a different time, drag the centre of the green bar to a new position along the Timeline
- To **shorten** the audio, click and drag either end of the green bar inwards

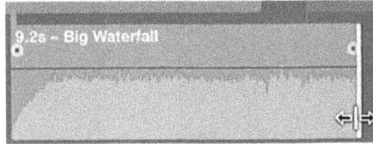

- To **adjust the volume,** drag the horizontal line, which runs the length of the audio clip, up or down to adjust the clip volume

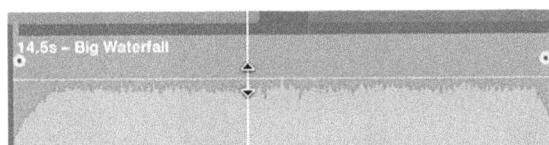

- To **fade the sound** in or out, drag the dot at either end inwards

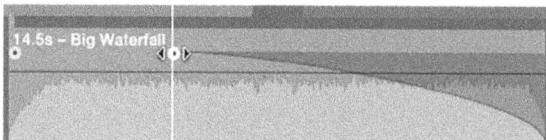

- To make a **custom adjustment to the volume**, hold OPT and click on the volume line to add an edit point. Drag this point up or down to the required volume. CTRL-click to delete edit points.

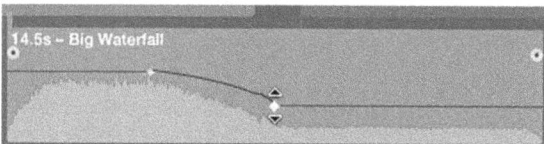

This is what the finished stop motion movie may look like in the Timeline.

Adding backgrounds (if required)

iMovie has a range of backgrounds including solid colour, animations and maps. They are useful under titles and some can be used on their own.

- Click the Backgrounds button at the top of the Browser ❷

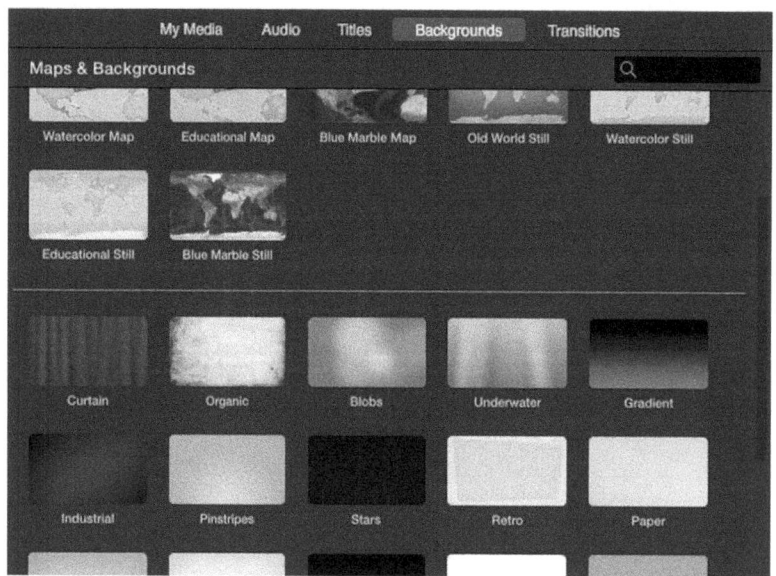

- Scroll the Browser window to see all the styles
- Drag the background into the Timeline ④ and place it before, after or between clips. Backgrounds are initially 4 seconds long.

To change the duration of the background, drag either end of the clip to the length you want.

Adding images (if required)

To import a photo or graphic (JPG, PNG or TIFF formats):

- Click the Import button ⬇
- Make sure the appropriate Event is listed at the top of the window
- Select the image, or select a connected camera and record a photo
- Click Import Selected – *the image is added to that Event*
- Select the image in the Browser ❷
- Drag the photo to the Timeline ④ to create a 4 second clip.

If you don't want to store a copy of the image in the Event Library, drag it directly from the desktop into the Timeline ④.

To change the duration of the image, drag either end of the clip to the length you want.

Images are automatically given a zoom effect called *Ken Burns*. If you want to change the effect or turn it off, double-click the image in the Timeline and change the style.

Create images for your logo or other branding graphic to add to your movie.

Adding transitions (if required)

Transitions are the way that the pictures in one scene close to reveal the first pictures in the next scene. Some iMovie transitions are simple, like 'fade to black'. Other iMovie transitions are more sophisticated and animated. If you have selected a theme for the movie you can also choose additional theme transition styles.

To fade from black at the start or fade to black at the end of the movie click the Settings button in the top right of the Timeline.

- Click the Transitions button at the top of the Browser ❷

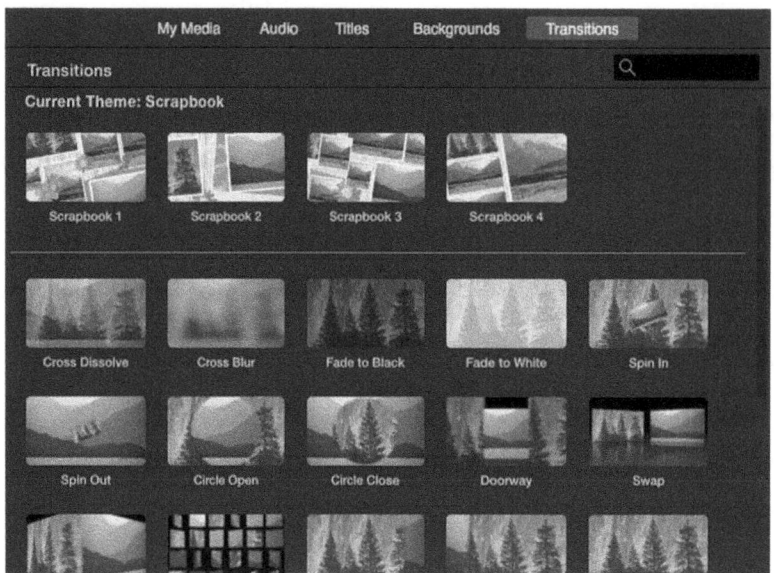

- Move the cursor over the transition styles in the Browser ❷ to see its animation effect. Scroll the Browser window to see all the styles. The most common transition in big screen movies is a straight cut (no transition) or a short cross dissolve
- When you have chosen the style you want to use, drag it into the Timeline ❹ between clips. Transitions are initially 1 second long
- Double-click the transition icon to change the duration of the effect.

Adjusting the clip

The Enhance button offers to assess and automatically optimise the colour and sound of clips. Select clips in the TImeline and click the button. If you don't like the enhancement, click the button again to turn it off for that clip.

There are a number of additional edits that can be made to the stop motion or a scene:

- Select a clip in the Timeline ❹
- The top of the Viewer ❸ has editing controls such as:
  - Changing the colour
  - Cropping the clip
  - Audio changes to audio volume and effects
  - Changing the speed and reversing the clip
  - Adding a video filter.

These edits apply to the whole clip, so if the scene you want to change is part of a larger clip you'll need to split it. Position the playhead in the Timeline and select Modify⟶Split Clip (CMD-B).

Assembling a larger stop motion project

iMovie has many more features for editing more complex movie projects. If your stop motion pictures were recorded in several iStopMotion files, or by several groups, use iMovie to edit them all together, such as in the following example.

Notice these features:

- The first clip is one of iMovie's animated backgrounds for the title with a short (1 second) transition to the first stop motion clip
- The last clip is iMovie's solid black background with a long (4 second) fade to black transition for a smooth effect
- There is no transition between other clips. Although, in another project, additional stop motion pictures could be recorded at the start and end of each clip to allow for transitions
- The audio of the stop motion clips has been muted and replaced by the full length soundtrack audio to run seemlessly across all clips. Before muting the clips make sure the clip audio aligns with the soundtrack to maintain sync.

179

Saving the movie

iMovie automatically saves movie projects as you create them. However, when you have finished editing your movie you need to save it as a movie file. To do this:

- Click the Share button
- Select the option you want.

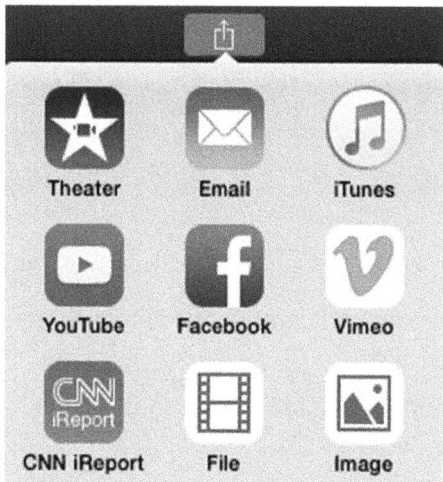

Each Share option has a number of settings to determine the size and quality of the file. For example, to save a movie file to the computer, enter the name, description and tags relating to the stop motion content. Select the resolution – either the same size or a smaller size and the quality. Refer to the estimated file size to make sure the resolution and quality will give you the file you want.

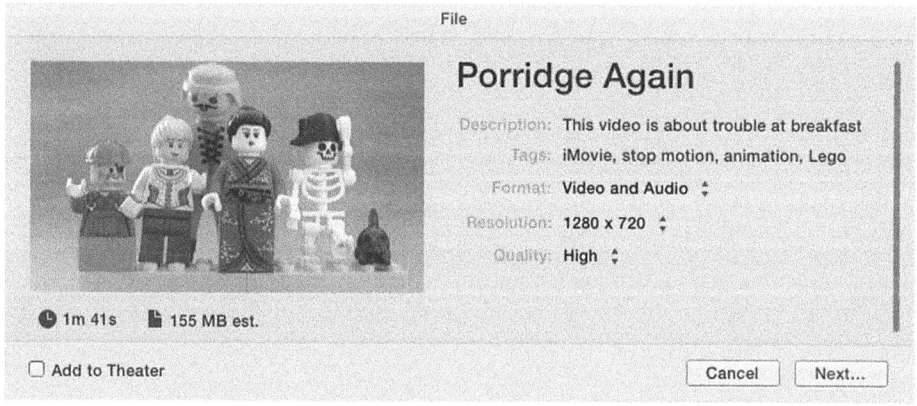

Websites for more information

Stop motion
www.aardman.com
www.stopmotionanimation.com
www.stopmotionworks.com
www.stopmotioncentral.com
www.shortoftheweek.com/channels/stop-motion
www.pesfilm.com
www.notsonoisy.com
www.newtownmovieschool.co.nz

Clay stop motion
www.clayanimator.com
www.animateclay.com
http://clay.s5.com
www.zombie-pirates.com

LEGO® stop motion
www.brickfilms.com
www.bricksinmotion.com
www.nightlynewsatnine.com

Whiteboard stop motion
www.thersa.org/discover/videos/rsa-animate

Search in Google or YouTube for *'stop motion'* for lots of examples of stop motion.

Premiere

If you've decided you want a special first screening of your movie, be sure to:

- Invite as many people as you can
- Choose the biggest screen you've got access to
- Connect some big speakers
- Shut the curtains
- Start with the speeches - thank your guests for coming, tell them about the movie and the people who made it, but don't say what happens
- Hand round the popcorn
- Turn off the lights and press play.

Index

Symbols
2D 11, 78, 148
3.5mm phono (connector) 34, 35
16:9 (widescreen) 109. *See also* widescreen
30° 122
720p 109, 115, 126, 155, 160
1080p 94, 109

A
AAC (file format) 50
Action safe (iSM) 88, 127, 146, 153.
    See also overlay *and* Title safe
acts. *See* parts (of a story)
Add Selection button (iMovie) 172
Add Track button (GB) 51
advertisement 31
AIFF (file format) 12, 50, 61, 118
alpha channel 155
ambience (sound) 44, 64
ambient noise 56. *See also* noise
Apogee 35
Apple Jam Packs (loops) 65
armature 11, **75**
artificial light 100. *See also* lighting
atmosphere (sound) 63
audio 12, **33**, 34, 35, 36, 50, 53, 57, 59, 60, 68,
    71, 123, 127, 128, 129, 178. *See also* soundtrack
    and sound
    Audio/MIDI 51
audition 43
auto focus (AF). *See* focus
Automatic Level Control (GB) 53, 54, 55, 57
automation (GB) 46, 68, 69, 70
Autosave (iSM) 115
Average Joe 76, 78

B
background 80, 81, 82, 83, 84, 85, 90, 91, 92, 122
    green screen 82, 156
    iMovie 176
    invisible horizon 81
    one-piece 81, 143
    painted 80, 91
    three dimensional 84, 85
    wide stage 81, 143
Backgrounds button (iMovie) 170, 176
back light 100, 101. *See also* lighting
battle 16, 62, 138, 144
beep during time lapse (iSM) 150
bitrate 61

Blair Preston 133
blurry (picture) 85, 89, **90**, 91, 97, 121, 125, 151,
    152. *See also* focus
bounce board 100, 101, **102**
brickmation. *See* LEGO
brightness 96, 101, 117
Browser.
    iMovie 170
    See also Media Browser *and* Loop Browser
Built-in microphone 35
Built-in output 51

C
camera 33, 91, 112, 159. *See also* focus
    and remote camera
    choosing for stop motion 94
    mount 98, 99. *See* mount
camera angle 80, 83, 84, **88**, 122, 153, 166.
    See also composition
chroma (green/blue) 82, 156
claymation 10, 11, 187. *See also* Plasticine
close-up 94, 96, 97, 122, 143, 144. *See also* macro
Colour correction
    iStopMotion 97, **117**, 151
    iMovie 178
Compositing button (iSM) 155
Compositing pane (iSM) 113, 155
composition (picture) 80, **86**, 87, 127, 160, 166
compression 49, 50, 61, 126
compressor (GB) 49
condenser (microphone) 34
contrast (iSM) 151
copyright 32
Count-in (GB) 40, 53, 67
Creative Commons 62, 63, 64

D
depth of field 89
dialogue 20, 23, 29, 36, **41**, 43, 44, 46, 52, 53, 57,
    58, 69, 122, 129
diffuser 100, 101, 152, 154
digital still camera 94, 121, 159
dimmer 101
Disney 58, 133, 164
DSLR 116. *See also* digital still camera
duct tape 79, 80, 103
dynamic (microphone) 34

E
editing
    GarageBand 46, 66, **68**, 69, 70, 71
    iMovie **171**
    iStopMotion 106, **126**, 139, 157, 158, 162
Editor (GB) 39, 54, 68, 69, 70
effects. *See* sound effects *and* Plug-in effects

184

Enhance button (iMovie) 178
Event (iMovie) 171
export
    GarageBand 71
    iStopMotion 71, **126**. *See also* Share file
        images 111, 117, 151, 158
exposure 94, **96**, 101, 116, 117, 152

F

file name 12
fill light 100, 101. *See also* lighting
film - look like a 90
Firewire 95
fisheye 95
flood (light bulb) 101
focus 80, 97, 117, 141
    auto (AF) **89**, 152
    fixed 95
    manual (MF) **89**, 91, 94, 95, 116, 143, 147, 148, 152
    Tilt shift 151
foley sound 61. *See also* sound effects
foreground 84, 85, 155
FPS (frames per second) 109, 110, 111. *See also* picture rate
frame rate 109, 115, 149. *See also* picture rate; *and* FPS (frames per second)
full screen
    iMovie 174
    iStopMotion 123

G

gamma 117
GarageBand **36**, 37
genre 65
genres 17
green screen 82, 156
Grid (iSM) 127

H

headphones 36, 57
helpers (iSM) 158
hero/ine 17, 21, 22, 27
high definition (HD) 94, 109, 115, 126, 155
how to make
    2D Plasticine characters 78
    armature Plasticine character 75
    camera mount 98
    microphone 'shock' mount 59
    portable stage 104
    remote camera mount 99
humour 16, 138

I

iGlasses (webcam settings) 94

image stabiliser 94
iMovie **170, 171**
Import images (iSM) 111, 117, 151, 158, 161, 162
Import button (iMovie) 171, 177
improvise (script) 18, 23, 26, 58
Inspector (GB) 39, 40, 47, 52, 53, 54
Instrument. *See* Real Instrument *and* Software Instrument
instrument (musical) 36, 64, 65, 67
    USB 45, 67
intensify (iSM) 151
invisible horizon background 81, 143
iOS device. *See* remote camera
iPad, iPhone or iPod Touch. *See* remote camera
iPhoto 60, 162
iSight 95, 150
iStopCamera app (iSM) 95, 116
iStopMotion 50, 71, **108, 113**, 115, 126, 161
iTunes 36, 44, 60, 61, 170
iTunes button (iMovie) 174

J

JPG (file format) 156, 176

K

keyboard
    built-in (GB) 36, 67
    musical 36, 45, 61, 65, 67
    track (GB) 44, 45
key light 100, 101. *See also* lighting

L

LCD display (GB) 38
LED lights 96, 101
LEGO 10, **79**, 80, 94, 95, 97, 99, 104, 110, 121, 130, 131, 132, 134, 136, 137, 138, 139, 164, 166, 187
Libraries (iMovie) **170**, 171, 172, 174, 176, 177
Library button (GB) 38
Library (GB) 38, 44, 45, 52, 67, 71
lighting 82, 96, **100**, 101, 102, 103, 110, 116, 117, 126, 141, 152, 153, 156, 166. *See also* exposure
    artificial 100, 152
    back light 100, 101
    fill light 100, 101
    key light 100, 101
lip-sync 127, 128
Logitech webcam 35, 94, 99
Loop Browser button (GB) 38, 45, 65
Loop Browser (GB) 38, 45, 61, 64, 65, 66
loops 36, 44, 45, 56, 64, **65**, 66

M

M4A (file format) 50
macro 94, 95, **97**
manual focus (MF). *See* focus

Mattel 28
Media Browser button (GB) 38
Media Browser (GB) 38, 45, 60, 71
    Audio tab 60
    Movies tab 60
mega-pixel 94, 160
Metronome (GB) 40, 53, 67
microphone 33, **34**, 35, 36, 40, 41, 42, 44, **51**, 52, 53, 54, 55, 56, 57, 58, 62, 65, 69
    3.5mm phono (connector) 34
    omni-directional 34
    shock mount 59
    uni-directional 34
    USB 34, 35
    XLR (connector) 34, 35
MiniDV 95
mistake 57, 68, 122, 152, 153, 157, 161, 162
mono recording (GB) 52, 53
mount 140
    camera **94**, 98, 99, 122, 137, 146, 147, 148, 152, 160
    microphone 34, 57, 59
mouth shapes 57
MOV (file format) 12
movie competitions 29
MP3 (file format) 36, 45, 50, 61, 118
Mr Potato Head 133
music 32, 36, 38, 43, 44, 45, 46, 49, 51, 53, 56, 60, 61, 62, **63**, 64, 67, 70, 71, 118. *See also* copyright, Royalty free; *and* Creative Commons
    iMovie 170, 174, 175
music score 67, 70
music video 15, 122

N

noise 34, 43, 44, 45, 53, 54, **56**, 57, 59, 61, 68, 69, 70
    ambient noise 56
    versus sound 56
Noise Gate (GB) 49
non-musical 36
NTSC 109

O

offset (iSM) 119, 128, 129
Olloclip 95
onion skinning (iSM) 127
orientation (iSM) 123, 148
    lock 123
overlay (iSM) **127**, 135, 136, 140, 142, 149, 160. *See also* overlay slider
overlay slider **113**, 114, 122, 127

P

PAL 109, 155
parts (of a script) 27
parts (of a story) 21, 22, 26
phoneme 133
Photoshop 158
piano roll (GB) 70
picture rate 109, 110, 111, 112, 162. *See also* FPS (frames per second)
picture size 94, **108**, 109, 111, 126
pictures per second. *See* picture rate
pitch (audio) 47, 49, 70
Pixar 21, 29
Plasticine 10, 11, **74**, 76, 87, 110, 133, 138, 140, 148, 154, 164, 166
    2D character 11, **78**, 148
    armature 11, **75**
    modelling tools 74
Playback checkbox (iSM) 129
playhead
    GarageBand 41, 53, 67, 68, 69, 158
    iStopMotion **114**, 121, 123
playlist (iTunes) 61
plot cards 20
Plug-in effects (GB) 46, 47, 48, 49
PNG (file format) 155, 156, 158, 176
poems 24
portable stage **104**
precise editing 69
Preferences
    Garageband 51
    iStopMotion 108, 115, 150, 155, 158
premise 19
preset (iSM) **108**, 109, 115, 126, 155, 161, 162. *See also* picture size
Preview Area (iSM) **113**, 116, 117, 123
Preview button (iSM) 121
principles of animation 164, 165, 166
project (iMovie) 170, **171**, 172, 179, 180
pronunciation 58, 134
protagonist. *See* hero/ine
PSD (file format) 156

Q

Quicktime 36, 126

R

Real Instrument (GB) 36, 51, 65. *See* track
Record button
    GarageBand 42, 53, 67
    iStopMotion 119, 120, 121
recording
    audio **2**, 18, 51, 61, 62, 65, 67. *See also* sound quality

pictures **4**, 71, 111, 113, 114, 115, 119, 120, 121, 160. *See also* time lapse
Recording button (iSM) 116
Recording pane (iSM) 113, 116, 148, 151
Record Level (GB) 40, 53, 54, 55, 57
reference video 114, 127, **128**, 129, 135
remote camera 95, 99, 116, 123.
 See also iStopCamera app
 lens 96
 mount 98, 99
 settings 117
remote shutter release 159
reverse order (iSM) 126, 140
rotate set 84, 136, 154
Rotoscope (iSM) 127
royalty free 32, 44, 45, 62, 64
Ruler (GB) 38, 53, 67
rules 122
 rule of thirds 87, 127, 153

S

saturation 116, 151
Save file
 GarageBand 40, **50**, 71
 iMovie **180**
 iStopMotion 115, 123, **126**, 161, 162
script 15, 16, **19**, 23, 24, **26**, 41, 58, 159
 advertisement 31
security system 150
shadow 100, 101, 102, 103, 126, 146, 147, 148, 153, 163. *See also* lighting
Share file
 GarageBand 50, 71
 iMovie 180
sharpen 151
shotgun (microphone) 34. *See also* microphone
sidebar 113
single frames 119
skeleton. *See* armature
slide show 119
Smart Controls (GB) 39, 47, 52
Software Instrument (GB) **70**. *See also* track
Solo (GB) 47, 68
sound 33, 35, 36, 45, 52, 53, 54, 55, **56**, 57, 60, 66
 quality 54, 55
 versus noise 56
sound effects 36, 44, 60, **61**, 175
 instrument 61
Sound Effects button (iMovie) 174
sound quality 33, 53, 56, 57, 61
Sound recording process 42
soundscape 44, 64
soundtrack 2, 12, 33, 36, 38, **40**, 46, 49, 50, 68, 71, 114, 118, 127, 174

editing 68, 70, 71
Soundtrack panel (iSM) 71, 118
Source panel (iSM) 116, 123
South Park 21
speech. *See* dialogue
split clip (iMovie) 177
spot (light bulb) 101
Stabile Coil 98
stage 79, 80, **81**, **82**, 84, **85**, 86, 87, 92, 95, 97, 98, 100, 101, 122, 141, **143**, 153, 156. *See also* background
 portable stage 104
 scale 83
 wide 81, 143
stand 34. *See also* mount *and* tripod
status bar 114
stereo recording (GB) 52, 53
still camera. *See* digital still camera
stinger (music) 63
story **16**, 18, 19, 21, 27, 28, 29, 43, 58, 97, 110, 122, 141, 144, 153, 166
 story outline 20, 21, 22
storyboard 114

T

talk (animating) 132, 133, 134, 135
themes 28
 iMovie 171
theme tune 63
thumbnail (iSM) 114, 117, 118, 121, 123, 126, 128, 158, 162
TIFF (file format) 155, 156, 176
Tilt shift (iSM) 151
time lapse (iSM) **112**, 119, 120, 150
Timeline
 GarageBand **38**, 71
 iMovie 170
 iStopMotion **114**, 118, 121, 126, 128, 162
tint 116
title and credits 12, 106, 118, 119, 121, 123, 124, 127. *See also* titles
 audio for 43, 46
Title safe (iSM) 127. *See also* overlay *and* Action safe
Titles button (iMovie) 170, **172**
titles (iMovie) 171, 172, 173, 179
Toolbar (iSM) **114**, 116, 118, 119, 127, 155
track (GB) 38, 41
 software instrument 45, 61, 65, **67**, 70
Track header (GB) 40, 41, 42, 46, 51, 53
transition 141
 iMovie 171, 177, 179
Transitions button (iMovie) 170, **177**
transparency. *See* alpha channel
transport controls (iSM) 114, 121

trim (GB) 43, **68**, 69
tripod 93, **94**, 97, 98, 122, 146, 148, 149, 159, 160.
   See also mount
TV 31, 32, 58, 94, 109

U

unbalanced 34
underscore (music) 64
uploading photos 161
USB 34, 35, 36, 45, 67, 94
   webcam. *See* webcam

V

video 109, 126. *See also* music video
   and reference video
   effects 178
video camera 35, 95, 116
Viewbase 98
View button (iSM) 118, 127
Viewer (iMovie) 170, 177
View pane (iSM) 71, 113, 118, **127**, 128
voice 36, 37, 43, 47, 51, 52, 58, 65.
   See also dialogue
voice-over 132. *See also* narration
voice actor 53, 57, 58
volume
   GarageBand 38, 41, 43, 46, 49, 53, 54, 63, 68,
      69, 70. *See also* automation
   iMovie 176, 178

W

walk (LEGO) 130, 131
Wallace and Gromit 133
waveform (audio) 39, 53, **54**, 118, 123, 127, 128
   Show Waveforms button (iMovie) 172
WAV (file format) 61, 118
webcam 35, 94, 116
Webcam Settings 94
white balance 94, **96**, 116, 117, 146, 147, 148, 152
whiteboard 11, 79, 133, 142, 147, 148, 154, 166,
   187
wide angle 95, 143, 150
widescreen 109, 155
Workspace (GB) **38**, 44, 45, 60, 65, 67, 71
written (script) 23, 24

X

XLR connector 34, 35

Y

YouTube 11, 64, 109, 146, 147, 149, 151, 163, 187

Z

zoom (camera) 83, 95, 156
zoom (magnification)
   GarageBand 38, 68, 69, 70
   iMovie 173, 175
zoom (microphone) 34

Teacher lesson plans

This book contains comprehensive information about a wide range of topics relating to making stop motion. When used in a classroom, teachers can easily derive lesson plans for curriculum activities. The following pages outline some possible lesson plans.

1. Write a 3-part story which develops a premise
2. Write a story into a script
3. Write the script for a 30 second TV advertisement
4. Create a plasticine character
5. Create a set at scale
6. Record a soundtrack in GarageBand
7. Record stop motion pictures in iStopMotion
8. Animate a LEGO® character to walk
9. Animate a character to talk
10. Dramatise an action sequence
11. Develop an interactive whiteboard illustration
12. Create a time lapse
13. Add a title and credits in iMovie

Most activities can be undertaken in groups of up to three students.

Each lesson plan contains:
- A list of required prerequisites, equipment and resources
- Time allowance. Increasing the time will allow students to focus on quality improvement
- References to relevant pages in this book
- Suggested areas for assessment.

Stop Motion Handbook – Lesson Plan

Write a 3-part story which develops a premise

Learning area: English narrative development

Requires paper, pen and a copy of table on page 22*.

Allow 60 minutes.

Lesson plan reference

- Page 16; Whole group discussion on the importance of a story
- Page 19, step 1; Working individually, or in groups of up to three, write a premise
- Page 19, step 2; Brainstorm questions which develop the premise
- Page 20; Write the story in three parts. Hand out copies of the story outline table on page 22*. Students need to write at least one sentence for each of the seven prompts.

> ### Key things to assess
> - Originality of premise
> - At least one sentence for each of the seven prompts in the story outline
> - Logical idea development.

*You can download a copy of the story outline at *stop-motion-handbook.com/downloads.html*

Stop Motion Handbook – Lesson Plan

Write a story into a script

Learning area: English narrative development

Requires completed story outline from Lesson 1, paper and pen.

Allow 60 minutes for a one minute movie. Adjust for longer movies.

Lesson plan reference

- Page 23, step 4; Take the 3 part story outline developed in Lesson 1 and write the story into a script. Students need to determine the characters, locations, actions and lines of dialogue to support dramatising the story

- Guide students on script parameters, for example:
    - include at least three characters with speaking lines
    - no more than 2 locations (this will simplify artwork requirements)
    - movie duration (this will determine the length of the script). A one minute movie should have 8-16 lines and fill about half a page. A five minute movie could fill 2-3 typed pages.

Key things to assess
- Accuracy of interpretation of story outline from lesson 1
- Character development
- Meets stated script parameters.

Alternative task

Take a well known story and write the script in the style of a particular genre (see page 17). For example - *Cinderella* as a spy movie, *The tortoise and the hare* as a romance.

Stop Motion Handbook – Lesson Plan

Write the script for a 30 second TV advertisement

Learning areas: English, Arts, Social Science

This is an alternative exercise to develop a script. It requires writing that is both clear and brief.

Requires paper and pen.

Allow 60 minutes. Full completion of the stop motion advertisement (Lessons 3 to 7) could be achieved in around 4 hours (thirty seconds of stop motion using 12 pictures per second is only 360 pictures). Adverts should be self explanatory and don't need titles. Add credits for all adverts after the last one.

Lesson plan reference

- Group discussion on TV advertising
- Page 31, steps 1 to 4; Guide students on product or service parameters, such as:
  - something to promote healthier lifestyle
  - something to make you richer/save money.

  The goal of most advertising is to convince someone of their need to buy a product or service. It can be a fun and challenging task to advertise something that no one wants, such as cobwebs, traffic jams, cat pee, dirty socks or teachers.

For presentation, use iMovie to edit together all class advertisements into a 'commercial break' as they would appear on TV.

Key things to assess

- Suitability of product or service for stated guideline
- Persuasiveness of proposed benefits
- Realistic and practical artwork requirements
- Script can be read in less than 30 seconds.

 *Stop Motion Handbook – Lesson Plan*

Create a Plasticine character

Learning area: Arts

Requires art working space, wire, Plasticine, beads, modelling tools (see pages 74-75). Students may need supervision with use of bonding agent for armature.

Allow 60 minutes.

Lesson plan reference

- Page 75; Make an armature for a character and then mould it with Plasticine. The character should be able to stand balanced and have some limb movement (see also examples and tips on pages 76-77).

Key things to assess

- Solid construction and ability for some limb movement
- Ability of character to stand balanced
- Good use of colour, detail and overall presentation.

Stop Motion Handbook – Lesson Plan

Create a scene set in scale

Learning areas: Arts, Maths

Requires art working space, art materials and access to camera, tripod and stage. Younger students may require supervision with scissors for cutting cardboard.

This exercise assumes that characters (LEGO®, Plasticine or other) for the stop motion have been created.

Allow 60 minutes.

Lesson plan reference

- Pages 83; Temporarily set up stage and camera. Look through camera and mark the maximum height, projected character head height and horizon area on background
- Pages 80-85; Create the artwork for background and props in the same scale as the character.

Key things to assess

- Appropriate size and proportion of background detail when viewed through camera
- Appropriate scale between characters, props and background
- Good use of colour, detail and overall presentation.

Stop Motion Handbook – Lesson Plan

Record the soundtrack in GarageBand

Learning areas: Computer skills, Arts, Music

This activity can be achieved with students in the group taking turns to record the voices of each other, or with a helper to operate GarageBand, so all students in group can focus on their voice role.

Requires a recording space (see pages 56-58), microphone and computer with GarageBand (see pages 33-35). Students with musical ability could use USB keyboard or guitar.

Advanced students can be assessed to set up recording location with the criteria on pages 56-58

Allow 1-2 hours to complete 1 minute soundtrack. Adjust for longer soundtracks, those which make significant use of sound effects or require music composition.

Lesson plan reference

- Group discussion on general topic of music copyright and specific guidelines for use of music in soundtrack (see page 32)
- Page 33; Group discussion on questions at bottom of page
- Page 41-50, steps 1 to 8; with reference, as required, to pages 36-71.

Key things to assess

- Clarity of speech
- Appropriate tone and passion of voices
- Appropriate selection of music and sound effects
- No use of music without copyright clearance
- Minimal unwanted and background noises.

Stop Motion Handbook – Lesson Plan

Record stop motion pictures in iStopMotion

Learning areas: Computer skills, Arts

Recording stop motion pictures is best done with longer sessions because of the set up time required. If you have an area that can be left set up, students can make progress with a series of shorter sessions.

Requires:
- soundtrack from Lesson 6, or other source
- a room with tables where lighting can be controlled
- stop motion stage set, characters, backgrounds, props, camera, tripod and computer with iStopMotion.
  See pages 94-103 for set up of camera and lighting.

Hands-on experience of simple animation effects is a valuable learning exercise before completing the first movie.

Allow 1-2 hours per 30 seconds of movie, plus set up time.

Lesson plan reference

- Page 108; Pre-recording checklist
- Page 115-126, steps 1 to 8; Making a stop motion.

See also pages 86-93 (picture composition), 113-114 (using iStopMotion), 136-145 (creating visual effects), 152-154 (avoiding common mistakes).

Key things to assess

- Image composition. Good use of manual focus
- Good camera movements to dramatise the story and follow the character who is talking. Steady camera at all other times
- Appropriate character movements
- Consistent lighting
- Minimal common mistakes (see pages 152-154)
- Logical file naming system (see page 12).

 *Stop Motion Handbook – Lesson Plan*

Animate a LEGO character to walk

Learning areas: Computer skills, Arts

Making a character walk is a fundamental skill for using LEGO® in stop motion. It can be adapted for other character mediums.

This skill can be incorporated into an actual movie, or as a list of prescribed activities: walking, running, dancing, moon walking, dodging bullets '*Matrix*' style, turning around and slow walk, or whole body expressions, such as showing surprise.

Requires stop motion stage set, characters, camera, tripod and computer with iStopMotion.

Allow 60 minutes.

Lesson plan reference

- Pages 130-131.

See also pages 128-129 to use a video recording as a reference for movements.

Key things to assess

- Realism of movement
- Hand and head movements
- Integration with props, eg picking something up.

Stop Motion Handbook – Lesson Plan

Animate a character to talk

Learning areas: Computer skills, Arts, English

Can be used to dramatise a poem or text extract, instead of a story.

Requires stop motion stage set, characters, camera, tripod and computer with iStopMotion.

Requires a soundtrack with narrative or spoken lines, from Lesson 6, or another source.

This skill can be achieved as a specific activity (allow 60 minutes) or incorporated into a larger movie.

Lesson plan reference

- Pages 132-135; Communication is a fundamental skill for making movies, and more important for stop motion because all visual clues to the dialogue must be produced by the character's ability to talk. The range of possible and appropriate mouth movements will depend on the medium used for the character
- For scenes with a number of characters talking refer to Rule 1 and Rule 2 on page 122.

See also pages 86-91 for information on picture composition.

Pages 128-129 to use a video recording as a reference.

Key things to assess
- Convincing lip sync
- Good camera movements to follow story and the character who is talking.

Stop Motion Handbook – Lesson Plan

Dramatise an action sequence

Learning area: Computer skills, Arts

Knowing when to move the camera, and when not to, are key skills for creating stop motion (see Rule 1 and Rule 2 on page 122).

This activity is to choose an active sequence (such as sport, battle, dance, race to build a tower, Plasticine art formations) and to move the camera as much as possible, to engage the audience in the flow of the action, while maintaining good composition and story flow.

Requires stop motion stage set, characters, camera, tripod and computer with iStopMotion.

This skill can be achieved as a specific activity (allow 60 minutes) or incorporated into a larger movie.

Lesson plan reference

- Page 143-144

See also pages 86-91 for information on picture composition.

See 'Rule 2' on page 122.

Key things to assess

- Image composition
- Good camera movements to follow the action in the story
- Steady camera and stage at all other times
- Appropriate character movements
- Consistent lighting
- Minimal common mistakes (see pages 152-154).

Stop Motion Handbook – Lesson Plan

Develop an interactive whiteboard illustration

Learning areas: Computer skills, Arts

Whiteboard stop motion is a quick start process as it does not require the preparation of characters and backgrounds.

An internet search for *'whiteboard stop motion'* will provide many inspirational examples of a whiteboard as a medium for stop motion art.

Requires whiteboard and markers, camera, tripod, computer with iStopMotion.

Allow 60 minutes, plus additional time to create a soundtrack (Lesson 6).

Lesson plan reference

- Page 147; A whiteboard can be used as:
    - a medium for telling a story with a soundtrack
    - an expression of moving art with a music backing added later.

Key things to assess

- Logical evolution of character shapes
- Useful or clever inclusion of other elements, such as a hand appearing to create or stretch certain elements
- Picture composition and use of screen area
- Steadiness of board and camera.

Stop Motion Handbook – Lesson Plan

Create a time lapse

Learning areas: Computer skills, Science, Arts

Requires camera, tripod and computer with iStopMotion.

This is best done over a period of hours, but depending on the topic could be a much longer duration.

Lesson plan reference

- Page 112; Set up a camera in a vantage point to record a process for observation and analysis:
    - chemical reaction such as a melting ice block, water evaporation
    - nature study such as a flower opening, butterfly hatching
    - study of movement such as traffic queues at different times of day, people waiting for a bus, tracking shadows across playground.

See also example on page 150 which uses time lapse as a security system.

As a variation in visual style see Tilt Shift example on page 151.

Key things to assess

- Interesting choice of subject matter
- Suitable camera angle and camera settings
- Appropriate picture rate (FPS) for purpose.

Stop Motion Handbook – Lesson Plan

Add a title and credits in iMovie

Learning areas: Computer skills, Arts, English

Requires completed movie and computer with iMovie.

Allow 60 minutes.

Lesson plan reference

- Page 171-174; Add a title sequence and credits to an existing movie.

Key things to assess

- Spelling
- Appropriate style of title and credits to support the movie and not overpower it
- Final movie exported with same picture size as original iStopMotion movie.

www.ingramcontent.com/pod-product-compliance
Ingram Content Group UK Ltd.
Pitfield, Milton Keynes, MK11 3LW, UK
UKHW050415240426
12048UKWH00021B/1527